S0-AZE-965

A Singular Life

A Singular Life

Perspectives on Being Single by Sixteen Latter-day Saint Women

Edited by
Carol L. Clark and Blythe Darlyn Thatcher

Deseret Book Company
Salt Lake City, Utah

Printed in the United States of America

Library of Congress Cataloging-in-Publication Data

A Singular life.
Includes index.
1. Single women—United States. 2. Single women—United States—Religious life. I. Clark, Carol L., 1948– II. Thatcher, Blythe Darlyn.
HQ800.4U6S56 1987 305.4'890652 87-22269
ISBN 0-87579-107-7

First Printing October 1987

From CLC
To my dear sister, Alice Elaine Clark Cannon,
with thanks for all the joy you bring to my life
And to MarJean Clark Wilcox and Elaine Low Jack
true friends

From BDT
To all who have my heart, especially Kathleen Eyring,
Barbara B. Smith, Sharon B. Swindle, Emma Lou Thayne, and
Mary Beth Clark, for greatly enriching my writing and my life,
and Kenneth R. Madsen, whose sun has not even
begun to set . . .

Contents

Preface

The authors in this volume are widely diverse in career choice, educational background, geographic location, and age. What they have in common is their commitment to the gospel of Jesus Christ.

This book will prove an invaluable contribution to all Mormons, no matter what their marital status, for it reflects the challenge and the joy of striving to live the gospel more fully. As editors, we learned much from our sisters' perspectives. Just as each author is unique, so each chapter is refreshing, enlightening, and sometimes humorous.

We commend this book to all Mormon women and men who love this life and strive to live it well.

What Does This Situation Require?

Jeanie McAllister

I have always loved horizons. Give me the ocean rolling against an unbroken sky, or an airline window seat above the clouds, or the tallest skyscraper from which to see the city lights, and my mind can feast for months on memory pictures.

Perhaps that's because I grew up with wonderful horizons. Many nights I watched the full moon rise above the canyons of my childhood, flooding the warm summer grass until it seemed like day. And when it was too late to stay outside, I would run inside, strike the house lights, draw the curtains, and sit in the darkened living room to watch the moon's command performance.

In those days, the horizons of my life stretched ahead of me, clear and uncomplicated. But as years went by, life grew more complex and uncertain. By my late twenties, I had left what I'd once considered a permanent career in public teaching and was working in Nantes on the western seacoast of France, trying to determine what my next steps should be.

Jeanie McAllister is a management development specialist. In that position she has traveled widely to conduct management training seminars. She earned a bachelor of arts degree in French and political science from Brigham Young University and a master of arts degree in British and American literature from the University of Utah. She has done postgraduate work in children's literature at Ohio State University. Her Church callings have included a variety of leadership and teaching positions in the auxiliaries.

During many nights that autumn, I had to cross an acre of pitch black field to catch the nearest bus into town; and often as I walked, the words of the hymn came into my mind:

> Lead, kindly Light, amid th' encircling gloom;
> Lead thou me on!
> The night is dark, and I am far from home;
> Lead thou me on!

(*Hymns of The Church of Jesus Christ of Latter-day Saints*, 1985, no. 97.)

These words always gave me courage. I often sang them in the darkness, praying not only that I was headed in the right direction toward town but also that my life was headed on the right course because I truly could not see what lay ahead. And I was a lot farther from home than France.

In the years since, this experience has become a metaphor for my life. Oh, that I could see even a little into the distance to what the future holds. Instead, I see "through a glass, darkly" (1 Corinthians 13:12), one step at a time, and this pattern promises to continue. As a single Latter-day Saint woman with a deep conviction of eternal marriage and family, I'm attempting to fit the puzzle of my life together with major pieces missing—a more than ambiguous process.

"Why is a nice young woman like you still single?" people have often asked me through the years. And although my replies have been sometimes scintillating and other times serious, I have yet to discover a truly satisfactory answer to that question myself. What I *have* discovered is that "Why?" is the wrong question. Viktor E. Frankl's words first helped me to understand that. Speaking of the horrors of life in a concentration camp, Frankl says: "We had to learn . . . that it did not really matter what we expected from life, but rather what life expected from us. We needed to stop asking about the meaning of life, and instead to think of ourselves as those who were being questioned by life—daily and hourly." (*Man's Search for Meaning: An Introduction to Logotherapy* [New York: Pocketbooks, 1963], p. 122.)

As a single woman, whenever I have replaced the question "Why is this experience happening to me?" with the question "What does this situation require of me?" I have discovered specific actions, the doing of which has prevented my derailment and kept me pushing along the path, even in the darkness. Unmet expectations may be bitter, but I want to be better for my experiences; and the difference between *bitter* and *better* is *I*. I can choose not to be immersed in bitterness. Asking "What does this situation require of me?" helps me see that I can make choices. I can control my life, even if that control extends only as far as my perceptions and attitudes.

Over the years, then, these are some of the answers that come again and again when I ask, "What does this situation—being single—require of me?"

This Situation Demands That I Begin

Begin a new relationship. Begin a new neighborhood. Begin a new career. Begin a new financial commitment. Even though some puzzle pieces are missing, I must start putting together those that do fit. It is so easy when single to delay making major decisions. A single woman decides not to invest in a home, for example, because she might marry and move away or because it seems so permanent, forgetting that every home here on earth is temporary. The single woman's knowing who and when she will marry certainly would help many other decisions fall into place, but without that knowledge, she must begin wherever she can make a step.

Beginning is a way to overcome the paralysis that the unknown often brings. Novice writers are taught to overcome writer's block by scrapping detailed outlines and starting to write any place they choose. If they have ideas for the middle of a composition, then they are encouraged to start there. This strategy also works in life's ambiguous or flat periods. As I put one foot in front of the other, moving along, eventually the landscape ahead begins to come into focus.

Besides experiencing ambiguity, a woman who has been single for a long time may go through a certain mourning period—mourning for a companion never known, for children never born, for time passed never to be recaptured. For widows, mourning periods are publicly acknowledged, whereas single never-marrieds experience this period privately and without the memories of a loved one or the certainty that someone awaits them on the other side.

But as Ecclesiastes says, there is "a time to mourn, and a time to dance." (Ecclesiastes 3:4.) At some point, the single woman must call an end to the mourning and start the dancing. In the words of Broadway's irrepressible Auntie Mame, she must

> Open a new window, open a new door,
> Travel a new highway that's never been tried before
> . . . .
> There's only one way to make the bubbles stay,
> Simply travel a new highway, dance to a new rhythm,
> Open a new window ev'ry day.

("Open a New Window," words and music by Jerry Herman [New York: Jerryco Music, 1966].)

At one point in the play, Mame tells her nephew Patrick that life is a banquet and some poor fools are starving to death. By choosing to find something delicious in each experience rather than bewailing what's not on my plate, I can always feast. And I must begin.

This Situation Requires That I Make a Friend of Time

Time for the single woman is often viewed as an enemy, especially as the infamous biological time clock ticks on. In our world of instant results where meals are microwaved in seconds, how do we learn to deal with blessings promised "in due time"? In the framework of the gospel, a single woman who is keeping the commandments sees immediate results from obeying the Word of Wisdom or the law of tithing, and yet the blessings she may yearn for most seem completely out of reach.

I have found that one of the answers is to focus on the present. *Now* is the only real time there ever is. When a child newly arrives from heaven, it takes several years before he or she grasps the mortal concept of time. Could it be that children are so carefree because they are so oriented to the present?

The present is a peaceful place where we need not worry about past mistakes or future fears. People who fear commercial flying are taught to train their minds to think only of the present moment, not of what might or might not happen during the remainder of the flight. I, too, can do something right now that might seem overwhelming if I thought I had to do it forever. It is impossible to live years within minutes, but we try to do it all the time when we fail to focus on the present and become obsessed with the future.

And yet we sometimes must think of tomorrow. As fearful as the years ahead may seem to the single woman growing old alone, the future can also become a friend if viewed properly. Frankl tells of getting through some of his most difficult moments in the concentration camp by imagining himself years hence, sharing with an audience what he had learned from his present sufferings.

Looking for future meaning in present situations is a technique that has helped me keep going many times when I have found myself tiring. This technique is actually the gospel principle of faith, because it requires me to exert my mind to envision a reality in the future that I cannot see in the present. In contemplating the friendly use of present and future, I like to think of the tightrope walker who, with perfect balance, keeps his eyes on the future goal, all the while aware of the present process of placing one foot in front of the other.

But what are we to do during those times when the present seems too painful and the future bleak and comfortless? We may look productively to the past. I love the little poem that says:

> There was a Dachshund once so long,
> He hadn't any notion
> How long it took to notify
> His tail of his emotions.
> And so it happened
> While his eyes were
> Filled with woe and sadness,
> His little tail went wagging on
> Because of previous gladness.

Remembering "previous gladness" and past times when we received the Lord's blessings can give us infusions of strength to meet present challenges. Before meeting Goliath, David looked back, saying, "The Lord that delivered me out of the paw of the lion, and out of the paw of the bear, he will deliver me out of the hand of this Philistine." (1 Samuel 17:37.)

Of his arduous mission to the Lamanites, Ammon recalled: "Now when our hearts were depressed, and we were about to turn back, behold, the Lord comforted us, and said: Go amongst thy brethren, the Lamanites, and bear with patience thine afflictions, and I will give unto you success. . . . Now behold, we can look forth and see the fruits of our labors; and are they few? I say unto you, Nay, they are many. . . . blessed be the name of my God, who has been mindful of us." (Alma 26:27, 31, 36.)

We are told, "Count your many blessings. . . . / And it will surprise you what the Lord has done." (*Hymns*, no. 241.) Recalling the past helps us to see that while we thought the Lord was not walking by our side, yet we were carried unknowingly in his arms through some of our darkest hours. This is one important reason why we are counseled to keep journals. They help us remember faith-promoting experiences from the past, giving light and hope when neither seems to be shining brightly before us.

Past, present, future—all seasons may prove friendly if we use them wisely. Time is what turns grass into milk. Time is what makes patience possible. And our exercise of patience helps the Lord to work his will in our lives without our getting in the way.

This Situation Entreats Me to Exercise Faith

Faith is that spiritually aerobic practice of hoping for things "which are not seen, which are true." (Alma 32:21.) *Exercise* is the perfect verb to use with faith because it implies continual practice as life adds heavier and heavier weights, making our spiritual muscles grow more capable of bearing burdens.

What can I do to exercise faith? I can concentrate on what is certain. That is not easy in our age of uncertainty. A college degree does not guarantee a lifetime job. A jumbo jet does not guarantee a safe arrival. A temple marriage does not guarantee a faithful partner. We make decisions that seem certain and secure but can be undone in a moment by change, collision, or catastrophe.

Yet while we are living in the most uncertain of times, we are also living in the most certain—a time when the gospel is here in its fulness, a time of prophets and promises, both to us as a people and to us individually. If I view my life at times as a puzzle, I must also remember that my patriarchal blessing is the picture on the lid of the box. "What greater witness can you have than from God?" (D&C 6:23.)

A woman who has waited much of her life for promised blessings, however, sometimes finds herself believing she must have done something in the past to nullify those promises. Sometimes she simply stops believing altogether because it is less painful. What can she do to exercise faith if she finds herself in this situation?

She can thank the Lord for those blessings promised in her patriarchal blessing but not yet received—those things "which are seen, which are true." I have learned that thanking the Lord in advance makes me more alert to blessings when they do come and has increased my faith that others, only mentioned, will yet come to pass.

Although a patriarchal blessing usually covers the broad sweep of our lives, extending beyond mortality, it is not necessarily comprehensive. It is important to remember that we may receive blessings not detailed there. For instance, the specific promise of posterity was never mentioned to my mother, yet she gave birth to five children and has twenty-five grandchildren. Often, many years after receiving a patriarchal blessing, we are given additional light and knowledge in other priesthood blessings because the Lord knows that what we have experienced in the interim has better prepared us to be recipients.

To exercise faith I can also live righteously. *Lectures on Faith* tells us that "unless [the saints of God] have an actual knowledge that the course they are pursuing is according to the will of God they will grow weary in their minds, and faint." (Joseph Smith, *Lectures on Faith* [Salt Lake City: Deseret Book Co., 1985], pp. 67–68.) I used to wonder how I could know if the career path I was taking was acceptable to God. Then one day I realized that the path I should concern myself with most must always be the path of righteousness, and the Lord will help me in the places where I cannot see far ahead. The scriptures tell us that "the path of the just is as the shining light." (Proverbs 4:18.) Security does not consist of knowing what lies outside us or ahead of us; security lies inside us when we are close to him.

Concentrating on what is certain, giving thanks for blessings, and living righteously all increase our faith. Nevertheless, even when we are trying to do our best, fearing that blessings may not come will weaken what faith we have been able to develop. Fearfulness is not of the spirit of the Lord. "For God hath not given us the spirit of fear; but of power, and of love, and of a sound mind." (2 Timothy 1:7.) Fear works against us. And when we give it haven in our hearts, we may find ourselves in the same position as some early elders in the Church who were told, "Ye endeavored to believe that ye should receive the blessing which was offered unto you; but behold, verily I say unto you there were fears in your hearts, and verily this is the reason that ye did not receive." (D&C 67:3.) If I find myself in this situation, it demands that I discipline my mind to focus on the task at hand rather than on the fear itself.

A wonderful example of such focusing was shared with me by Hazel Hilbig, a special education teacher who taught reading to elementary school children of varying grade levels. She routinely gave her students practice tests to alleviate their nervousness when they faced an actual reading test. But one of her students had failed many times and was experiencing emotional trauma at home. During his practice test he began to read with quivering lips and halting voice. A young Korean boy, just learning English, was part of the group. Sensing his classmate's anguish, he turned and advised, "Don't scare. Just read."

These simple words remind me of an experience I had one December when I left graduate school and drove across the country alone in treacherous weather. Semi trucks were strewn along the freeway as I drove past Chicago. Three hundred people had been stranded in their cars by a fierce ice storm in Des Moines. The road I had traveled on was closed to traffic behind me just after I passed through Rawlins, Wyoming. I was driving with a fever and an aching throat, afraid to take medicine that would make me sleepy. The swirl of the snow across the highway made me feel as if I were at sea. I kept wondering what I would do if the weather caused something to go wrong mechanically with the car, if another driver should skid into me, or if I were stranded somewhere on the open plains.

I tried singing hymns to keep awake, but I needed something rousing to counteract the icy fear, my utter aloneness, and the quiet sameness of mile after mile of snow. Quite naturally the words to "The Lord Is My Light" came into my mind. "Then why should I fear? / By day and by night his presence is near. . . ." And the words to the second verse came just as easily. "The Lord is my light; though clouds may arise, / Faith, stronger than sight, looks up through the skies." (*Hymns*, no. 89.) Singing helped focus my mind. I tried not to scare, just drive. I remember promising in prayer that I would also drive fear from my mind, focus on the task at hand, and let the Lord "lead me, lead me along."

When I had returned safely home, I had to retain that focus of faith when I was again faced with determining new personal and professional directions for my life. After this experience, the words of the hymn I'd sung since childhood were forever changed for me. To this day, they bring a flood of emotion because I know that the Lord teaches us most powerfully through symbols, and my cross-country trip was both a literal and a symbolic preparation for other crucial life experiences to follow where I would need to look to him even more.

Fear may come not only from intense experiences but also from listening to others around us. For the single woman it may be voices that say, "It's too late," "You should have . . . ," "You're too fussy," "If only. . . ." Loud physical noise drowns out smaller sounds and can cause stress and debilitation; likewise, listening to voices other than God's voice, even if the voices are well meaning, can drown out the still, small voice, causing us to grow weary in our minds and faint.

Heavenly Father's voice of perfect mildness helps me focus my mind on faith. I love to hear him in the scriptures, saying:

"As I was with Moses, so I will be with thee: I will not fail thee, nor forsake thee." (Joshua 1:5.)

"Fear thou not; for I am with thee: be not dismayed; for I am thy God: I will strengthen thee; yea, I will help thee; yea, I will uphold thee with the right hand of my righteousness." (Isaiah 41:10.)

How to exercise faith is shown in the story of the famous trapeze artist who was teaching his students how to perform on the high trapeze. One young man froze with fear at the sight of the fragile bar above him and choked, "I can't do it." The instructor wisely replied, "Son, you can do it, and I will tell you how. Throw your heart over the bar, and your body will follow." (Norman Vincent Peale, *The Power of Positive Thinking* [New York: Prentice-Hall, 1952], p. 111.)

Through the years, throwing my heart over the bar has become a habit that has worked again and again for me. But what of the times in life when it seems virtually impossible to get either heart or body over the bar? The single woman is usually her own major source of physical and emotional support. As she grows older, she may also be the major source of emotional support for aging parents and for other single friends. Though a career may not be her first choice, yet she goes forth to slay her own dragons each day and returns to her castle alone each night. Sometimes she grows weary. Megatrials or the cumulative effects of minitrials bring their own brand of battle fatigue. Perhaps she has prepared for the 100-yard dash and finds she is in the middle of a marathon. If I find myself fatigued or heartsick in the middle of the race, what does this situation require of me?

This Situation Whispers That I Pray For the Comforter

The ministration of the Holy Ghost during times of trial is well described by President Rex C. Stallings of the Salt Lake Winder West Stake. "Part of our earthly progression is to experience pain and suffering and disappointments. The Holy Ghost was meant to comfort us *through* sorrow, not necessarily to remove the experience of suffering. We need to learn this; otherwise, during suffering, we may start to disbelieve the Holy Ghost because we still hurt."

President Stallings recalls that as a child he would often skin his knees in play and then bump the scabs off several days later. Running in tears to his mother, he would climb into her lap and feel her warm arms rocking and soothing him. "It didn't take the pain away," he says, "but it gave me comfort. And that's how the Holy Ghost works. He doesn't take the pain away, but he gives you comfort."

During those times in my life when my heart has not cleared the bar, praying for the Comforter has slowly but surely brought a peace and a subsequent strength to my soul I would not have thought possible.

The Comforter can also bring all things to our remembrance. During difficult times we may be reminded that every trial has its ending and that we determine by our response whether or not the ultimate outcome will be positive or negative. Since we pay for our experiences with ourselves, they become virtually priceless. The same rain that beats upon us is also watering our souls. And when the sun reappears, knowing that we endured well the storm is one of the greatest rewards we can experience.

We may exult as did Ammon, saying, "Behold, my joy is full, yea, my heart is brim with joy, and I will rejoice in my God." (Alma 26:11.) Or we may feel to say as did the poet George Herbert, who, having endured major disappointments in his life, marveled at God's goodness with these words in "The Flower":

> How fresh, O Lord, how sweet and clean
> Are Thy returns! ev'n as the flowers in spring,
>
> . . . .
>
> Grief melts away
> Like snow in May,
> As if there were no such cold thing.
>
> Who would have thought my shrivel'd heart
> Could have recover'd greenness?
>
> . . . .
>
> And now in age I bud again,
> After so many deaths I live and write;
> I once more smell the dew and rain,
> And relish versing: O my only Light,
> It cannot be
> That I am he
> On whom thy tempests fell all night.

When we feel burned out by trials or beaten by battle fatigue, the Comforter reminds us that God can "make weak things become strong." (Ether 12:27.) The shrivel'd heart can recover greenness and in age bud again, for "earth has no sorrow that heav'n cannot heal." (*Hymns*, no. 115.)

Finally, This Situation Asks Me to Believe in Miracles

One of my favorite stories about miracles is of three young trees who lived together on a hillside. They often talked about what each would like to be when he grew up.

One said, "Babies are the sweetest things in the world. I should like to be a baby's cradle."

The second spoke, "That would not please me at all. I should like to be a great ship so I might cross many waters and carry cargoes of gold."

The third tree stood off by himself in deep reflection. "Have you no dream for the future?" asked the others.

"No dream," he answered, "except to stay on this hillside and point men to God. What could a tree do better than that?"

Years passed, and the three small trees grew up to be tall and beautiful. One day men came to the hillside and cut down the first tree. But he was not made into a cradle. Instead he was hewn into rough pieces and carelessly put together to form a manger. "This is not what I planned to be," he sobbed heartbrokenly. "Shoved into this dark stable with no one but the cattle."

But Heavenly Father, who loves trees, whispered, "Wait. I will show you something." And he did.

For one night when God's Only Begotten Son was born, he was wrapped in swaddling clothes and laid in the manger. The manger quivered with delight. "In all my dreams I never thought to hold a baby like this," he said. "Why, I am part of a miracle. Truly, this is better than all my planning."

Years passed. And men came to the hillside and cut down the second tree. But he was not made into a great sailing vessel. Instead he became a tiny fishing boat owned by a man named Peter. "To think that my life has come to this," he complained unhappily. "Just a fishing boat."

But Heavenly Father, who loves trees, whispered, "Wait. I will show you something." And he did.

For one day on the Lake of Gennesaret, Jesus sat in the little boat and spoke to the multitude on the shore. He spoke words of such wisdom and light that the little boat listened eagerly. "Why, I am part of a miracle," he whispered, his heart full of wonder. "In all my dreams I never thought to carry a cargo like this. Truly, this is better than all my planning."

Months went by, and men came to the hillside to cut down the third tree. "I don't want to go into the valley," he wept, as the axe cut into his heart. But the men tore away his branches, hewed him apart, and fashioned his pieces into a crude cross. "This is terrible," he quivered. "They are going to hang someone. Oh, I never wanted this to happen to me. I only wanted to stand on the hillside and point men to God."

But Heavenly Father, who loves trees, whispered, "Wait. I will show you something." And he did.

For one day Jesus took up his cross and was led to a place called Golgotha where he was crucified between two thieves. Afterwards, his body was laid in a tomb. But at dawn on the third day when Mary Magdalene and the others came to the sepulchre, an angel met them, saying, "He is not here: for he is risen, as he said." (Matthew 28:6.)

And the cross began to understand. "Why, I am part of a miracle," he marveled. "Jesus' great mission was to give his life so that all who have ever lived on earth can one day return to God and live with him again. In all my dreams I never thought to point men to God in this way. Truly this is better than all my planning."

The woman who has been single for many years often finds herself in a situation similar to that of the three trees. "This is not at all what I planned on," she may think. For the early, easily married, finding a companion seems quite commonplace; but for the one who has waited, nothing seems more miraculous. The single woman must believe that Heavenly Father, who loves her, is whispering, "Wait. I will show you something." And she must remember that signs follow those that first believe.

God's miracles are often so different from what we expect. As I think of my life and the lives of my friends and family through the years, I believe that although God's timetable has usually been inexplicable, his miracles have been better than all our planning.

My family always supposed that my father would live to a ripe old age. His heritage was one of longevity. He was a healthy and robust man, a man without guile, a man of great compassion and love for people from all walks of life. But while serving with my mother in the mission field, he began to lose his memory and reasoning abilities. Like the three trees, our family had moments of grief and terror. All of us went through our times of questioning, of wondering what was happening and why it was happening to our father. I thought over and over of the statement, "Anyone who doesn't believe in miracles isn't a realist." (Attributed to David Ben-Gurion, former prime minister of Israel.) It was time for a miracle, and no one deserved one more than my father.

Though my family is scattered across the country, we have always remained close in spirit. On an appointed day, we all fasted and prayed earnestly that my father would be healed. And each of us received the calm assurance that he would be all right.

As months went by, however, instead of gradually improving, he grew steadily worse. The final diagnosis was Alzheimer's disease. One neurosurgeon likened the condition of his brain to that of a bright city whose lights, one by one, slowly blink out. Once a man with a brilliant mind, he no longer knew the names of his children. We watched him die a little each day.

The calm assurance that we had once interpreted as possibly a promise of healing now became Heavenly Father whispering, "Wait. I will show you something." And he did. The miracle was not that my father was healed, but that his illness revealed the pure person he had become through all the years as he had faced his trials with faith and forbearance and a happy spirit.

The miracle was that the disease in all its hideousness could not destroy the essence of what was truly my father. As his mental faculties eroded, his spirit grew more luminous, his ability to communicate love grew even stronger. All my life I'd heard him pray for the welfare of his family, mentioning each of us by name. Now when I heard him pray, his words were broken and his sentences incoherent, but the spirit of his requests that the Lord watch over us was unmistakable. I read with new eyes the scripture, "Likewise the Spirit also helpeth our infirmities . . . the Spirit itself maketh intercession for us with groanings which cannot be uttered." (Romans 8:26.)

Willa Cather wrote, "Where there is great love, there are always miracles. Miracles rest not so much upon faces or voices or healing power coming to us from afar off, but on our perceptions being made finer, so that for a moment our eyes can see and our ears can hear what is there about us always."

The miracle was what happened to each of us as a result of this seeming tragedy. Our perceptions became finer, our capacity to love expanded, our desire to remain an eternal unit grew stronger than ever before.

Last autumn I spent some time in New York City on business. On several nights I stood at the window of my darkened hotel room as if in a theater. I looked at Central Park, twenty-one stories below, a black patch of stage ringed with lighted skyscrapers, and watched as the full moon entered from the right to rise majestically above Manhattan.

The moon was a harvest moon, and it was October, a year since my father's death. I found myself thinking of how well he had responded to what life's situations required of him, of how his soul had shone more brightly as the darkness deepened around him, of how the miracles my family experienced had blessed each one. I thought, too, of another night in Gethsemane when the Savior responded to what his foreordained situation required and brought to pass the great miracle of the Atonement.

The moon shines because it receives light from the sun. How brightly we shine when the Lord is our light. When we respond affirmatively to what life's situations require. When we begin. When we make a friend of time. When we exercise faith. When we pray for the Comforter. When we believe in miracles.

Single or married, no one sees very far along the horizon in mortality. As we ask, "What does this situation require of me?" and act on the answers, we realize more deeply that putting the puzzle of life together is as important as the pieces or the outcome. Ambiguity helps us practice this process and thus develops in us qualities that certainty never could.

Phillips Brooks said, "Do not pray for tasks equal to your powers. Pray for powers equal to your tasks. Then the doing of your work shall be no miracle, but you shall be the miracle." (*The Best of Words to Live By*, ed. William Nichols [New York: *This Week* magazine, 1967], p. 63.)

God tells us his work and his glory is to bring to pass our immortality and eternal life. (See Moses 1:39.) In responding well, we help him in that work, for we may become as he is. And there is no greater miracle.

Waiting or Enduring?

Rebecca Coombs

Some time ago I saw Samuel Beckett's play *Waiting for Godot* and learned a valuable lesson that has enriched my life. In the play the two leading characters, Vladamir and Estragon, are two comical transients whose lives seem to go in circles. Even though they experience human emotions such as pain, tragedy, empathy, and joy, their lives never seem to progress. Rather than getting the most from their experiences, they always choose to wait for some mysterious character, Mr. Godot.

ESTRAGON: Let's pass on to something else now, do you mind?
VLADAMIR: I was just going to suggest it.
ESTRAGON: But to what?
VLADAMIR: Ah! *(Silence)*
ESTRAGON: Suppose we got up to begin with?
VLADAMIR: No harm trying. *(They get up)*
ESTRAGON: Child's play.
VLADAMIR: Simple question of will power.

Rebecca Coombs is the public affairs director for a large outdoor advertising firm, for whom she negotiates contracts and coordinates public service work. She previously served as a political consultant with the Utah Education Association. Formerly a student at Brigham Young University, she has continued her political science studies at the University of Utah. Her Church callings have included a full-time mission in London and service as a Gospel Doctrine teacher.

ESTRAGON: And now?. . . Let's go.
VLADAMIR: We can't.
ESTRAGON: Why not?
VLADAMIR: We're waiting for Godot.

(Samuel Beckett, *Waiting for Godot* [New York: Grove Press, 1978], p. 54.)

I wasn't surprised that at the conclusion of the play the transients were still in the same place. The elusive Mr. Godot never came.

Although the plot disturbed me (I prefer happy endings), I could relate to Vladamir and Estragon. At the time, I had just returned from a mission, and I was struggling with what I should do with my life. I felt like I was going in circles. On the way home from the play, I wondered if perhaps my frustration was caused by my waiting, not for Mr. Godot, but possibly for something or someone just as elusive.

From the time I was very young, I had always desired to become a professional as well as a mother. Even though my high school seminary teacher warned me that my future children would likely end up in a commune if I tried to blend a career and family, I had a firm belief that it could be done. But at age twenty-three, when the reality of being single was staring me in the face, I was a little panicked. I began to doubt my former convictions and felt the need to reassess my situation.

I was vacillating because past experience had taught me that achieving excellence in academic and professional circles involved risk. Although I strongly desired to achieve, sometimes accepting the associated risks frightened me, particularly when I felt that one of the risks was staying single. For example, during my first year in college I met a fellow in a political science class whom I was just crazy about. I flirted with him for three solid weeks before he asked me out. After that, we saw a lot of each other and were becoming good friends. Unfortunately, at the end of the semester when I received an A and he received a B, the relationship took a serious nose dive. I was in a dilemma, wondering if the tables had been turned, would our relationship have been different? I also wondered if achieving the A was worth losing a friend.

To resolve my dilemma, I had to rely on a long-term perspective. The real problem wasn't the political science grade but a problem of opposing wills. If I had pretended that the A didn't matter to me, I would have been lying. I couldn't pretend to be something I wasn't. And if this experience hadn't happened, there would have been other experiences that would have uncovered our true colors. The problem of opposing wills would have surfaced sometime.

Nevertheless, having an experience like this one reinforced my apprehension about the future. I didn't want to think that my moving ahead professionally might lessen my chance of getting married. Once again, a long-term perspective of the situation helped me over my hurdle. Mentally I created a new scenario where I was less aggressive in my professional pursuits. I envisioned myself putting my career on hold and baking cookies more often for boyfriends. I then asked myself, "Have you improved your chances of getting married?" The answer was no. Next I asked myself a second, more important question, "Are you happier?" Again, the answer was no.

Using this long-term perspective, I uncovered a bigger risk: being single without having achieved my professional goals. That risk was more disturbing than the risk of just being single. In fact, I no longer feel that being single is a tragedy. I have realized that although I do not have total control over my marital status, I have been granted power to develop my talents. The real tragedy will occur only if I allow my own fear to hinder my progression.

If I could single out one practical aspect of life that brings me joy it would be progression. I love a challenge. I enjoy being engrossed in a project that challenges my ability. While working as an escrow officer a few years ago, I was delighted when one client commented on how much he enjoyed doing business with me. I had been in the position for only three months, and before that I hadn't even known the definition of the word *escrow*. I had just been very zealous and read through thousands of real estate contracts, learning all that I could in a very short period of time. Although the work was difficult, I loved it because it was new and challenging. I've learned that I am a person who needs to be occupied continually. Right now a challenging career is the best way for me to answer that need.

I feel resolved about my decision to move on and accept the challenges of the business world, but I have occasionally experienced twinges of guilt about being single. Sometimes I have worried that I might be failing in my calling as a woman.

During these moments I have recalled every semiserious relationship I have ever had. Mentally I have put myself on trial to find negative behavior patterns that I might have been guilty of that caused these relationships to fail. Invariably I have found faults. But sometimes I have gone overboard with self-persecution. At those times, when I have approached Heavenly Father through prayer with the findings of my self-conducted trial, I have felt inspired to lighten up.

I rely heavily on the encouragement I receive from Heavenly Father. Without it, I wouldn't have been able to get past my occasional feelings of insecurity and guilt about being single or to know that my life is on track. One evening, when I was deeply concerned about the direction my life was taking, I approached Heavenly Father on the subject again. I needed to know that I had his approval. I will never forget how calm I felt after making a covenant with the Lord that if a right opportunity for marriage came my way, I wouldn't say no. Also, I promised that I would try to encourage relationships. Since that time, I haven't felt guilty about being single. I will simply let my life unfold as it will.

Heavenly Father has also given me a great deal of encouragement through priesthood blessings. Years ago, during my junior year in college, I was questioning my direction. I had just been called as a Gospel Doctrine teacher in my student ward. I prayed and fasted for a confirmation from Heavenly Father that my life was in harmony with his will. On the day I was set apart, my bishop, who had no knowledge of my personal struggle, was inspired to tell me in the blessing that I was where I was supposed to be and that I was doing what I should be doing. I was overcome with gratitude for Heavenly Father's love and care for me. I have had other such experiences since that time. I cannot adequately describe how thankful I am to know that Heavenly Father is concerned with my present happiness as well as my eternal well-being and joy.

By reasoning with myself and relying on the inspiration of Heavenly Father, I have been able to win the emotional battle about feeling comfortable as a woman in a business environment. In my progression as a professional, however, there have been many external conflicts that I dealt with in the past, and there are other conflicts that I must deal with in the present. Just because I decided to make my mark on the world did not mean that all companies would accept me with open arms, saying, "Darling, welcome home!" Though I find it hard to fathom, some companies have even questioned my being there at all. I have been in a number of job interviews with hiring officials who have told me that I was a very attractive young lady and that if someone hadn't already proposed, it would surely happen in the near future. Then when I would leave my job (as all married females do), where would the company be?

I've responded to this absurd bias in a number of ways. On one occasion I suggested to the hiring official that I ought to try his approach with my creditors. I could just imagine the conversation: "Gentlemen, I am so sorry, but please do not expect further payment. You see, I'm young and attractive, so I'll probably be getting married soon." Another time I wondered how the person interviewing me could know something I didn't, so I jokingly asked if I could please borrow her crystal ball. On yet a third occasion, I commented that the company must recognize my value if they were already afraid of losing me. Unfortunately, my humor was never fully appreciated, nor were my talents.

All joking aside, every time I have faced this irrational injustice I have been hurt. It seems so unfair for something that I have little control over to be held against me. On the most recent of these occasions, however, talking with a close business associate who has already been through this struggle was a lifesaver. My friend was able to heal my ailing ego with a good dose of realism. She pointed out that real life just isn't like life in Camelot. Judgments are not always fair, and situations do not always work out. Being an idealist at heart, I really didn't like hearing it, but I had to admit that it was accurate.

As the conversation continued, my friend reminded me that any smart businesswoman will minimize her losses and move on. That was easier to do when I looked at the situations from a different angle. I imagined being hired by one of the companies that had expressed concern about my young, attractive, female nature. If they were operating under that bias, I realized, they would probably never take my work seriously. When opportunities for promotion would arise, my name would probably not be the first to come to mind. I could see that too much of my time and energy would be spent trying to overcome the company's bias rather than moving forward. Viewing the situation that way, I thought, "Who needs it?"

Yet, I did need some successful working situation. Finding my niche in the professional world has been very time consuming. Some people have been fortunate always to know exactly what they wanted to be when they grew up. I have had to try a lot of things to discover myself and my talents.

After returning from my mission, I didn't finish my last year of college immediately because I was clueless about how I would like to use a political science degree. It wasn't until three years later, after I had dabbled in everything from real estate to computers, that I returned to school to finish what I had started.

I have really had to struggle to be where I am. I believe being single and forming a life-style different from the norm has intensified this struggle. There have been many times when I wondered if my professional goals were worth it. Only recently have I felt that I am beginning to achieve them.

As a part of completing my political science degree, I worked as a full-time legislative intern. My budget was so tight that it was necessary for me to stay with my parents so I could have that opportunity to intern. Because they lived in Utah County, I commuted daily to the state capitol, sixty miles each way. In the evenings I worked as a part-time sales consultant for a fitness organization to keep gas in my worn-out car that had a habit of stalling at the most inconvenient times. On one such occasion when my car was stalled, I was so discouraged that I dissolved in tears. I asked myself, "Why are you doing this? Why can't you just be married and live in the suburbs?"

But I realize now that my struggles have been worth it. My trials have given me valuable experience that has opened doors that would otherwise have been closed. Even during the years when I was trying to find myself, I was developing skills that I am now able to rely on. For example, I was able to use a valuable business skill the time my worst fear as a corporate recruiter was realized to the fullest. In general, a recruiter's job is to find dissatisfied employees from one company and align them with another company that offers more challenges and better compensation. This process is called a search. While on one search, I unknowingly reached the company president on the phone instead of his sales manager, with whom I wanted to talk about a possible job offer. I gave the president my whole pitch before I realized to whom I was speaking. I was suddenly very nervous. Then I remembered my boss telling me to "fake it 'til you make it." On this occasion I was shaking in my shoes, but I used her advice to help me through. I made a joke out of it by saying I supposed that if I had my own company, I wouldn't want to go to work for someone else, either. Before I had finished the conversation, the president wanted me to recruit for his company. Because of experiences such as this one, my confidence is stronger, so that I am not squeamish about making initial contact with people in power positions.

My struggles have also helped me discover many of my positive character traits. I know now that I can come through in a pinch. I have learned that I don't crack under pressure. My ability to reason and negotiate with others has been improved through challenges. While working through personal disappointments, I have demonstrated my faith and shown my Heavenly Father that I won't turn my back on the gospel just because things aren't going my way. Discovering these character traits within myself has been very encouraging, and consequently, my challenges haven't seemed quite so overwhelming.

My major weakness has been a lack of patience. In fact, sometimes my level of patience, especially with myself, could be compared to that of an angry hornet. Running into a few emotional brick walls has been the only means possible of changing this weakness into a strength. When I have been in a situation that demands endurance, I have had to at least pretend to be patient. My pretend behavior has progressed towards reality, and I am slowly getting the hang of it. In developing patience I have had to remember that achievement is a process, not a destination. Life hasn't been quite as difficult since I realized that no one expects me to be a complete success at age twenty-six.

Reading in Abraham one day, I found a scripture that speaks of the sun and moon being placed in orbit so as to create day and night. Of this process the scripture relates, "And the Gods watched those things which they had ordered until they obeyed." (Abraham 4:18.) I was intrigued by the word *until*. If something as basic as night and day had to go through a process before reaching perfection, then maybe there was hope for me, after all.

I suppose there are trials that I could have chosen to avoid, but my desire to progress has overpowered my fear of hardship. I love Richard Bach's thought: "There is no such thing as a problem without a gift for you in its hands. You seek problems because you need their gifts." (*Illusions* [New York: Del Publishing Co., 1977], p. 71.)

Seeing myself progress and overcome challenges has brought me the most happiness in life. I have also experienced a lot of joy through pleasant diversions along the way. I've been involved in theater projects that have consumed every spare moment while at the same time providing a great creative outlet. I always enjoy planning a dinner party. Providing exotic food and stimulating conversation has given me a good social outlet. Sometimes I have been involved in something a little more quiet, such as an intense reading project. I went through a phase where I wanted to read everything ever written by or about Aristotle. Being creative, interacting with others, and keeping my mind active seem to be the common threads in all my activities. I find these diversions stimulating as well as relaxing.

I used to be afraid that as I grew older and remained single, my opportunities to share the things I enjoyed would decrease. Thankfully, I am finding just the opposite to be true. I am always finding opportunities to expand my circle of friends. I believe people from all backgrounds want to share their lives. As I have developed friendships with people from different age groups and varied religious and social backgrounds, my life has been greatly enriched. I don't feel that anyone with an open heart needs to go through life alone.

If I had to choose any one period of the earth's history in which to live a single (or married) life, it would be right now. I am not aware of another time when more options have been available to women. I think of Sarah when she was dealing with the heartache of being unable to bear children. She really didn't have another alternative in her life. No one encouraged her to pursue a business career, obtain a law degree, or perhaps take up journalism. Sarah's options were to tend sheep or weave rugs. There were no shopping malls where she could escape for a few hours, have lunch with her friends, and spend Abraham's money. Even though she was able to travel throughout the Middle East (and it wasn't much safer then, either), she was always known as Sarah, the one with the curse. When I think of all the things that I can do with my life, I am very encouraged.

I don't know how long I am going to be single. My future joys and sorrows are also a complete mystery. I believe having to live with so much uncertainty is a large part of learning to endure to the end. That phrase, "endure to the end," has been used lightly so often that it may sound like a cliché. But I firmly believe that the principle of endurance that the prophets have taught from the beginning of time is not only a requirement for exaltation but also the secret to real happiness in this life.

I have learned that enduring is really the opposite of idle waiting. Endurance requires action. Waiting is mostly wishful thinking. The life of Nephi has been a marvelous example to me of what it means to endure. I see him as a man who faced incredible odds but who always came out on top of the situation. He possessed immense faith and an iron will. Enduring his adversity and challenge made him great.

By enduring, or continuing to move forward in whatever situation I may be in, I am finding peace and contentment in this life as well as preparing to realize my greatest desire, which is described beautifully in the words of a favorite hymn:

> Oh, that each in the day of His coming may say,
> "I have fought my way through;
> I have finished the work thou didst give me to do."
> Oh, that each from his Lord may receive the glad word:
> "Well and faithfully done;
> Enter into my joy and sit down on my throne;
> Enter into my joy and sit down on my throne."

("Come, Let Us Anew," *Hymns of The Church of Jesus Christ of Latter-day Saints*, 1985, no. 217.)

Bright Stars

Cheryl Ballard

One late winter afternoon, after a day of lecturing to business associates in Cape Town, South Africa, I retired to one of my company's offices to check for messages from the American home front and to review the day's events. After taking care of my business affairs, I settled back in a comfortable office chair and surveyed Cape Town's spectacular panorama of earth and sky, mountain and harbor.

My stay in that distant land had been thoroughly satisfying. Audiences had been responsive, company goals had been met, and I felt wonderful. My business travels had taken me to many places but none quite so beautiful as Cape Town and its surrounding area.

The sun was just beginning to set over the city's famous Table Mountain, and the shadows of the evening were slowly settling over its magnificent seaport. The view was absolutely breathtaking. The moment was so exquisite that the sensation was that of looking off the earth's end and beyond. It was one

---

Cheryl Ballard is a markets development and planning specialist with the health sciences division of a large international company, a position that has taken her to places worldwide to conduct conferences and seminars. She studied at Brigham Young University and the University of California at Los Angeles. Her Church callings have included various ward and stake leadership positions in Relief Society and MIA. She has also served as a Sunday School teacher and stake missionary.

of those moments in life that we choose to hold close and treasure forever.

A sweet sense of peace and gratitude engulfed me, and I was immediately reflective. I wondered to myself how it is that life's journey had brought me here, to this moment, to this place.

In my reflection, my thoughts journeyed homeward to my small town beginnings, to strong roots and keen memories. Surely it was only yesterday that I had graduated from high school. Like so many other yearning adolescents reaching for adulthood, I had shouldered a huge collection of expectations—then rich with timetables certain to guarantee fulfillment and salvation's promise—expectations precious to me still but now molded, rearranged, and refined by life's experiences. Those experiences were marked with mercies and miseries, with moments of great joy and moments of great sadness, with wonderful opportunities and earned fulfillments—but with no marriage, no eternal mate.

A career had never been a priority; it was simply a necessity. Yet here I was, on a professional fast track halfway around the world, reviewing the steps of my life and its unexpected design. I found myself deeply grateful for what I knew of truth and its promises, for the peace of the moment, and for a life's curriculum that was so uniquely mine.

As the sun set over Cape Town and the beautiful lights of the city, harbor, and heavens began spreading the colors of night, I reflected further on home, beginnings, and childhood perceptions. As a little girl I had loved to sleep out under the stars. Many summer nights found me on the lawn snuggled in my old sleeping bag, looking up at the heavens. As I lay there in the quiet of night, I imagined in my child's mind that surely the brightest stars were the residing places of my loved ones who had passed on and were, perhaps, the abode of loved ones yet to come to earth. I paralleled bright star status with valiant living and determined in my young heart to live valiantly and achieve bright star status so that one day I could share celestial light with those loved ones.

Since those childhood days, reaching for the stars has come to mean many things to me. I have determined that refining our own light is our life's purpose. And, of course, I, like so many, have come to understand that refining is not a solitary process.

We need other bright stars to help us capture the light, understand whence it came, and increase and radiate that light within our own lives.

One bright star, Veon Riggs Shupe, a revered and long-time friend, frequently reminded me in my youth that "God did not just throw us out into space to flop around. He gave us every ingredient for greatness that he possesses. He gave us a span of time, he gave us limitless opportunities, and he promised that we need never be alone if we would seek his companionship and remain teachable." She counseled my friends and me to choose confidantes carefully and prayerfully and not to seek advice unless we were willing to take it. She admonished us to refrain from habitually rehearsing our tribulations, cautioning us that if we did, we would likely bleed to death emotionally and spiritually and become undesirable to our associates. Veon, a widow, was so filled with light, life, enthusiasm, fun, and good humor that we never doubted her. Her own example encouraged us to enjoy, not simply endure, the scenery of life. So it is with bright stars. Their light is contagious, and their influence immeasurable.

Another bright star, Joyce Everett, at twenty-six years of age was stricken with acute myelogenous leukemia. I had only a brief acquaintance with her in our ward before her husband found employment in another town. Shortly after their move, her leukemia was diagnosed, and she was sent for treatment to the UCLA Medical Center where I worked. I was also serving as a counselor in Relief Society at the time and so was asked to advise our ward members how best to serve her needs.

Stopping by Joyce's room every morning before work, during my lunch breaks, and each evening before going home became my routine. At first, it seemed there was little I could do to ease her great physical and mental suffering. Although we were close in age and had been in the same ward, she was married, the mother of two children, and I was single. A bonding between us was not immediate. We had first to establish a common ground where the blessings and blending of our sisterhood could flourish.

The days of her hospitalization dragged into weeks. My daily visits continued with little evidence of benefit until gradually the light of sweet friendship began to dawn. The blending of spirit and need, of comfort and confidence, began to bless our association. Our conversations became open and ongoing; we spent our energy and tender emotions planning strategies for making every moment count. We understood, as never before, the value of time, of precious relationships, of gospel truths. We grieved over the social barriers that had kept us from knowing one another until tragedy struck and its circumstances finally forged an eternal friendship we would otherwise never have realized.

The evening Joyce Everett died, some eighteen months later, her life's star was radiant. Her faith was secure, and she welcomed mortality's wondrous sequel. My exposure to that radiant spirit greatly enhanced my desire for further light. I prepared for and then received my temple endowment. Soon after, I was called to be an ordinance worker at the Los Angeles Temple. What a great privilege it was to stand before those brides, young and old alike, and utter the promises of eternity. I came to realize that nothing was worth compromising that eternal moment in the temple, that tender understanding of life, its purposes, promises, and responsibilities. It was a cherished realization in that young season of my life.

Although I was still comfortably situated in an office chair in Cape Town, my thoughts remained in Los Angeles. I remembered the time I had just been called to be the Relief Society president in a singles ward. My counselors and I were thoroughly enthusiastic about our callings. Young and inexperienced, we yearned for the wisdom to perform our duties properly.

The year 1976 was approaching, and we wanted to plan something spectacular within the framework of Relief Society to celebrate our country's bicentennial. As a presidency we determined that Sister Belle Spafford, the recently released general president of Relief Society, could vitally affect the success of our plan. She had served as president for nearly thirty years and was revered by women the world over. Her tremendous understanding of issues affecting the women of the Church and the world at large, coupled with her dynamic ability to interpret those issues and communicate answers to them during that trying time for Latter-day Saint women, was convincing evidence that she could singularly ensure the achievement of our goal. Sister Spafford accepted our invitation, and our lives were never quite the same thereafter.

How well I remember sitting in the car with her while we waited for some of the sisters to arrive. She turned to me and said, "Sister Ballard, what is it your women need to hear? What can I do for them? How can I help them?"

I said, "Sister Spafford, the single sisters of this area, like so many worldwide, need to have a purposeful identity. We need to know that our lives count, that married or single, our destinies can be rich and fulfilling and acceptable to the Lord. We need to know and understand that single life can be a treasure and an opportunity to nurture and bless in ways that we may not think of because we are so consumed with our singleness."

She thought for a moment and then reached across the seat of the car, took my hand, looked me directly in the eye, and said, "Sister Ballard, don't you worry, and don't you let your young women worry. The only thing that is important in this life is that you endeavor to make your contributions of the highest quality. If you will do that, you will fulfill your destiny, and you will realize the blessings of eternity."

She went on to tell me, "Yes, many of you will have marriages and raise prosperous families. Others will have duties that lie mainly in the area of public service or public well-being. It matters not, only insofar as you endeavor to make your contributions of the highest quality. This is a new day and a new age where we need strong, available, capable, righteous women to carry our womanhood so that extremists will not run away with it."

That was a very poignant moment for me, a moment that has mattered greatly in my life's unfolding. In her address that evening, Sister Spafford gave the same counsel to the women gathered there. She afforded us all a worthy focus and a new flexibility. She gave me, personally, much more freedom to perform the tasks at hand; her counsel enabled me to contribute wisely and to further balance my expectations. And so another bright star, a brilliant star, had come to show me the way, to light my path.

The hour was growing late. South Africa's sky was heavily star-laden, reminding me of the land of Israel where I had visited only months before.

Since childhood I had envisioned with unbridled wonderment the great encircling glow of Bethlehem's magnificent star that had marked the birthplace of the Savior of the world. In

Israel, standing with my traveling companions in Shepherd's Field, reviewing that long ago scene, the profound significance of my childhood fascination with bright stars became clear.

The light of a new and bright star had announced the birth of the Savior of the world. (See Matthew 2.) The Savior called himself the "bright and morning star." (Revelation 22:16.) The scriptures are replete with star imagery—no wonder my childhood yearnings for bright star status held such promise! The words of William Wordsworth filled my mind, expanding my star imagery:

Our birth is but a sleep and a forgetting:
The Soul that rises with us, our life's Star,
  Hath had elsewhere its setting,
    And cometh from afar:
  Not in entire forgetfulness,
  And not in utter nakedness,
But trailing clouds of glory do we come
  From God, who is our home.

(Ode: Intimations of Immortality from Recollections of Early Childhood.)

As I had pondered the heavens from my hotel balcony in Jerusalem that night, I felt profoundly grateful for my life star and for the Home from which I came and to which I would return. I thanked my Heavenly Father for lending me the light of so many of his precious and bright stars, even his brightest, the Savior of the world. I realized anew that my experiences as a single woman had prepared me to deeply appreciate and comprehend the magnitude and meaning of that wonderful place and moment. I had no desire to lessen the moment by wishing my life otherwise. Still, I knew there was one essential and eternal companion star yet to appear in my heaven. I didn't know when that event would take place; I simply understood that it would.

Finally rising from my Cape Town office chair, I paused for one last, breathtaking view of my spectacular South African surroundings, especially the star-laden sky. Then I departed, closing the door on a wonderful evening of peaceful reverie.

The Odyssey

Carol L. Clark

I remember the exact moment I decided I wanted to marry. It was in the Cambridge Massachusetts Ward during a fireside. I was barely twenty-two. The speakers, George and Lenore Romney, had impressed all of us with their expertise, testimony, and poise. It is the poise I remember most because I so lacked it in those days. In that meeting something clicked, and I felt my first real longing to be part of a marital unit. I envisioned speaking tours and raising children and success—all in one clear, happy moment.

As we left the chapel, I followed the men I most admired—those in the ward I longed to date, and that day, also to marry. I listened as they lauded Lenore Romney and wished, loudly I thought, that the women in the ward even approached her in charm, intellect, testimony, and poise.

I was wounded. Although I knew no harm was intended, still, I was crushed. Their words seemed the most hopeless kind of indictment. "I can be like that," I remember thinking. "Look

---

Carol L. Clark is the Utah governor's special assistant for education and communications. In this position she serves as a senior policy adviser and liaison for public affairs. She holds a Ph.D. from the University of Utah in educational administration and has completed postdoctoral work at Columbia University Teachers College. A consultant and award-winning author, she is active in civic affairs and has held many positions in government and business. She served on the Relief Society General Board for eleven years and has filled numerous other Church assignments.

at me," every fiber of my soul cried. "I can *be* that." In my youthful earnestness, I longed for one of those men to turn and see the inner me, the woman I would yet become.

That day I attained a spiritual majority to match my legal passage into adulthood. I was terribly disappointed, yet I saw my own potential more clearly than I ever had before. I thought of myself as a real candidate for wifehood and motherhood, and my thinking about men and marriage has never been the same.

Paul's words fit that experience: "When I was a child, I spake as a child, I understood as a child, I thought as a child: but when I became a [woman], I put away childish things. For now we see through a glass, darkly; but then face to face: now I know in part; but then shall I know even as also I am known." (1 Corinthians 13:11–12.) In my twenty-third year I began my personal odyssey away from the glass, darkly, toward the light of personal responsibility and mature womanhood.

As I look back on that time, I sense that even then I began to unravel some truths about life: it's tough occasionally even for the poised, exacting always for anyone intent upon personal growth, and unfair intermittently for all God's children. Most importantly, as I turned my back on the glass, darkly, the thought budded in my heart that God is just and every experience in life has its place—even if I must reshuffle my life to find room for it.

Choose Life

The Saints are fond of saying, "Life is so short." As I age, I understand more fully what they mean. Still, I would respectfully submit that life is long enough.

When I am slogging through something, I just think life is long enough. Period. But most of the time I love life, and because I do, I am convinced it is long enough to invest in with energy, wit, heart, spirit, and strength. During my salad days when I was much greener in judgment, I often felt life was passing me by as I longingly waited for marriage. And how I longed. I pined over men, sighed away dateless weekend nights, and embraced fervently the myth that marriage would make me whole.

Throughout the entire decade of my twenties, most of my personal energy was spent in dealing with my frustrations socially and with my disappointment in not being a wife and mother. My view of life's continuum was hazy. Beyond wife and mother I had a hard time visualizing other meaningful objectives. It frightened me to ponder an adulthood devoid of the only two roles I thought a woman should have. In fact, I felt life owed me wifehood and motherhood. I had been faithful, my desires were right, so where was the husband?

I now see that much of the blame I placed on singleness for my insecurity was an unintentional scapegoating. I did not yet know how to face life squarely, just the way it is. For long periods of an entire decade, it was as if life politely presented itself to me on a silver platter, but rather than feasting upon the fruits there, I periodically shoved them out of the way and said, "I'll starve until I get what I want."

When I was a child, my beloved mother often played a record sung by John Charles Thomas. I recall lyrics of two songs in particular. One said, "I want what I want when I want it. That's all that makes life worth the while." The other began, "Roaming free as the breeze . . . I can roam as I please—open road, open sky." I came to love this music (I matured musically at twenty-two as well). I also related to both sets of lyrics. One side of me demanded that life give me what-I-wanted-when-I-wanted-it, that is, marriage by age twenty-eight. Another side of me eyed the horizon of an unexplored world and sought for the ways and means to adventure through life. I thought these goals were incompatible, so I wavered between them. When my mind was focused on marriage, there was no other goal, no other dream. When my mind was caught up with other pursuits, I felt I'd betrayed my quest for wifehood and motherhood. It took much experience for me to blend the goals, to sample the fruits from many platters with equal relish.

It also took a few dips in the crucible of experience for me to lose some rough edges about wanting-what-I-want-when-I-want-it. A scorching plunge into the crucible came when my only—and younger—sister married. I was twenty-seven and so, so single. She was twenty-five and marrying prince charming (a man who has in fact proven to be prince charming in every respect). This state of affairs shredded my theories about how things are supposed to be. I had expected I'd marry first. I didn't. That event brought me face to face with the fact that my wants and expectations were not necessarily the will of the Lord for me. In some cases they weren't even very plausible. I didn't like that lesson very much. But there it was, the truth that noble goals do not actuality make.

Through this and other experiences, I began to see my life not as a series of cause and effect relationships but as an odyssey. The advantage of such a perspective, I have found, is that with it all things seem possible. The uncharted nature of some phases of life is no longer menacing; in fact, it smacks of the adventure I only tasted in my twenties. I have learned that if one goal doesn't work, another one will. Each day becomes an unparalleled opportunity to do battle with my own weaknesses, to bask in the blessings the Lord has provided, and to try something new. Mine is a very comforting view of the world and a very motivating one.

I derive part of my credo from "Lucinda Matlock," a poetic epitaph. Lucinda, an ordinary woman, loved life and remonstrated with her posterity:

> What is this I hear of
> Sorrow and weariness,
> Anger, discontent and drooping hopes.
> Degenerate sons and daughters,
> Life is too strong for you.
> It takes life to love life.

(Edgar Lee Masters, *Spoon River Anthology*.)

And what is life? Moses had an answer for that. Here was a man who wandered in a desert for forty years with people who never put their lives together. As a bonafide antiflake, I sympathize with what must have been monumentally frustrating at times. In the book of Deuteronomy I have read Moses' words to the generation who would cross the river and inherit the promised land. There they stood, poised anxiously on the bank, and the aged prophet, who was not crossing with them, laid out the truth: "I call heaven and earth to record this day against you, that I have set before you life and death, blessing and cursing: therefore choose life, that both thou and thy seed may live: that thou mayest love the Lord thy God, and that thou mayest obey his voice, and that thou mayest cleave unto him: for he is thy life, and the length of thy days." (Deuteronomy 30:19–20.)

No footnotes, no disclaimers, no exemptions. To all those people Moses said the same thing: the options are clear; either darkness or light can be yours. So choose life!

I love the challenge Moses gave. I often think of my own life as a series of options, each choice leading me down another path. At the crossroads of two paths, I see in my mind's eye two signs, each reading "New opportunity" or "No longer an option." Some doors open, others close along the road I travel, yet even though marriage and family are not currently mine, choice is a daily companion on my journey toward the best that life offers.

The bottom line is that the light of the gospel is the opposite of the glass, darkly. Heading toward spiritual maturity means leaping with faith away from darkness and the causes of darkness: despair, loneliness, anger, disillusionment. Besides, what better adventure could there be than to truly live the gospel? I find that the light that enters my soul when I focus on the gospel infuses wonderful types of reality into my life. I still feel deep wells of longing for my husband and our children, but I more patiently accept my journey through life when I am spiritually in control, not in the midst of a spiritual tantrum because I still want-what-I-want-when-I-want-it.

I have come hard to this knowledge. I am a Joan of Arc type who still heartily hopes life will be good and pure and just. At twenty-two through the glass, darkly, I saw life as a series of scintillating events, each day a panoply of excitement and pleasure. I wanted crowds to jump out of subway cars singing and dancing, not pulling their belongings to them as they elbowed past slower fellow travelers. When jostled by testy passengers through mortality, I have often lamented that life just does not measure up to my glorious expectations.

Now a more seasoned traveler, I know that the real fun of life is in overcoming obstacles while still happily hoping everything will work out. Moroni reminds me, "Wherefore, whoso believeth in God might with surety hope for a better world, yea, even a place at the right hand of God, which hope cometh of faith, maketh an anchor to the souls of [women]." (Ether 12:4.)

My inherent gusto means I choose to be a "cockeyed optimist." I take Moroni at his word. Still, the fact is that my girlhood dreams have not come true. Should I lapse into terminal hysteria? manic depression? material obsession? misogamy?

Never! No one, nothing is going to ruin my life. I am the heroine of my odyssey, and I'll rise triumphant. My mettle has been sufficiently tested that I can say with surety, I will overcome anything. I freely admit that living with my dreams unfulfilled has proven to be a softening, humbling influence because it's been so hard. But the anchor is at hand, and because it is, I can progress, even though to date I've lost at love—the one thing I've wanted more in life than anything else save righteousness itself.

Awake, My Soul!

I am a thoughtful person, and there are times personally and professionally when I feel I'm living a Kafka story and people will turn into bugs or I'm part of a Salvador Dali landscape and a clock will melt off a table. Aspects of mortality, particularly Mormon singleness, baffle me. I do not have the answers in many cases. Sometimes I don't even have a clue; all this living as a single woman stuff can seem so strange.

But I have the driving desire to live well. I have wrestled with my personal demons and come to the simple conclusion that my life will be a good life. The journey to that decision was a long, arduous one, and I'm not to the end of it yet. But I am determined to be steadfast, even with all my fits and starts.

Last summer I complained to a non–Latter-day Saint friend that I was exhausted, having no fun, living like an automaton. Nonsympathetically, she countered, "What do you think this is? A dress rehearsal? This is your life, Carol. Fix it." I expected a pat and a kind word. Instead, I got a splash of reality square in the face. She was, of course, quite right. I wasn't giving my life value, so I didn't feel it had value. I went home, reread the parables of the sower and of the talents, and regrouped.

I decided the problem was that I was acting as if singleness had stolen my free agency from me. Time and time again I have had to remind myself that even if I were married, I'd have no fewer decisions to make than I do now. I join Nephi, who said:

"Behold, my soul delighteth in the things of the Lord; and my heart pondereth continually upon the things which I have seen and heard.

"Nevertheless, notwithstanding the great goodness of the Lord, . . . my heart sorroweth because of my flesh; my soul grieveth because of mine iniquities. . . .

"O then, if I have seen so great things, if the Lord in his condescension unto the children of men hath visited men in so much mercy, why should my heart weep and my soul linger in the valley of sorrow, . . . and my strength slacken, because of mine afflictions? . . .

"Awake, my soul!" (2 Nephi 4:16–17, 26, 28.)

Like Nephi, I am troubled by my own foibles and cognizant of my blessings. The critical element, however, is the awakening process: the trick to this single state is not to let the moments of self-doubt and foggy perspectives distract me for long. Nephi teaches me over and over that I must awake, and that is a conscious act on my part.

My physician, Homer Ellsworth, is also my friend. He gives me prescriptions for books as well as for medicine. He also taught me one of the most salient lessons I have ever learned about investing in life—the process of awakening. One day we were walking and talking about men. I was pouring out my concerns about being so single so close to forty. My friend responded, "Do you know what the major problem is with most single men and women? They are afraid to take risks. Life says, 'Go for it,' and they say, 'I'm afraid.' "

I reran my internal tape of decisions I'd made about marriage. I vowed that even if I went to my grave single, no one would ever say of me, "That Carol Clark just didn't have the courage to face life and to face herself." I looked at my own heart and vowed again that I would redouble my efforts to awaken to the spiritual realities. I decided to—

1. Create a "Someday I want to . . . " list as the first step toward a "This year I will . . . " list. Both lists provide direction and hope.
2. List what I like and dislike doing most. I will use this list as I make additional career decisions.
3. Renew old friendships and generate new ones. I am sending more postcards, holding more creative parties, and focusing my thinking on people rather than on work.
4. Enjoy male friendships more.
5. Take myself less seriously.
6. Take the gospel more seriously.

Adopt-a-Family

I do not believe in the weight-loss philosophy of marriage. That is the philosophy, often espoused, that if a woman will lose weight or change her hair or move to another city or sparkle at men, etc., etc., she will marry. For some of us getting married has never been so causal or so easy.

Here I am, in need of a family and without immediate access to the family situation I'd like. I know the problems related to not having husband and children, but what about the cures? Global catchalls like the weight-loss philosophy are not going to get me to the altar, and life races along. So what is to be done about this need to connect? The first step toward an answer is to think of family in some new ways.

I love my family, I dote relentlessly on my nieces and nephews, and sometimes, especially at Christmas, I feel like a fifth wheel. It is always painful to attend the family Christmas party alone. Surrounded by my married siblings and their children at the end of yet another year, I often feel the loneliest spirit of isolation. I join with the closest family I have, remembering I am not the closest family they have.

That definition of *family* is a vital distinction to me, and one I have discussed with some of my family. I believe it is easier for me to understand them than it is for them to understand me. They follow the pattern of the family in which we all grew up. I do not. I need them in ways they don't need me, and sometimes I sense the differences keenly.

My friend Elizabeth Haglund, who has been at this single game longer than I, once told me something that changed my life. I was complaining about the Christmas business, and she said, "Carol, if you don't have a family, build one." At first I thought she was telling me to care less about my own parents and my sister and brothers and their families, as if less caring generated less pain. I supposed she wanted me to fabricate relationships with friends' children as if I didn't need a family relationship of my own.

She straightened me out by explaining that years ago when she realized she would not have her own children, she knew her need for a close family relationship would not diminish just because her childbearing option was over. She made it a point to be part of her siblings' families and to "adopt" children of neighbors, ward members, and friends in ways that met their needs—and hers. Quite literally, she "built" a family who now absolutely adore her.

I have found her counsel to be wise. In the past, I often waited and hoped to be included in one of my sibling's family activities. I wanted to be needed, to be one with all of them. Too often I was disappointed. After Elizabeth's inspired counsel, I worked on my attitude. I decided I needed to do things differently, and I knew the entire responsibility lay with me, not with my family. Now I do the following:

1. Expect some moments will be uncomfortable. Standing alone on the back row of the family picture will never be my favorite, so sometimes I just do my best and leave it at that. Even when I am not comfortable, I try to remember to thank the Lord that I have a family I love. They love me too. Love is so rare a commodity that it should never be undervalued in whatever form it may be found.

2. Enjoy my parents. In the past three years I've taken one trip abroad each year with my parents. What adventures we've had! My relationship with my parents has broadened to a friendship few children ever know. My parents are my best pals, and we can have as much fun looking over an atlas in anticipation of a new expedition as most people have on the actual trip. We love to be together because we've taken the time to know one another. We have developed a unique, invincible mutual support system, for which I am daily grateful.

3. Keep in touch with my siblings. Raising children creates a different set of demands on my sister and brothers than my life-style has on me. While we are all equally busy, I have more flexibility in my schedule. I feel it is, therefore, my responsibility to go see them rather than waiting for them to come see me. I adore my sister and brothers. The best way I can communicate that is to be interested in them. I try to be steady in my relationships because although we might have more to talk about if I were married and rearing children, I would not love them any more if my life-style were more akin to theirs.

4. Love the children. I was saddened recently when a friend of mine complained that his nieces and nephews had ruined a family get-together by running around and making noise. Home is for peace and quiet, children are for delight—and that means noise and peanut butter on my silk blouse and lots of juicy

kisses. I spend as much time with my nieces and nephews as I can. I hope to be an Auntie Mame in their lives—a spark plug who introduces them to wonderful new worlds. Happily, they often introduce me to worlds either long forgotten or previously unexplored.

As an example, Clark, who is five, and I had a very serious discussion about the differences among trolls, elves, brownies, and fairies. This was a weighty matter for him, so I went home to find all my children's books with pictures of those delicious creatures I had so loved as a child. What fun to withdraw from the hard professional world I live in and to scurry around in his world of fantasy.

Jeffrey wanted dinner—now. I was amused by his four-year-old insistence and asked, "Jeff, don't you know about delayed gratification?" (As a single woman, I certainly do.) He pulled himself up to full height, looked me right in the eye, and said, "No, but I know New York."

Touché! I was put in my place. He was right—he knew many things I didn't, including how to imagine things I've never seen and how to dance as if summer lived in his legs.

5. Remember that relationships are not static. Friendships with family members ebb and flow as do friendships with others. I try to remember that things change. I may need companionship when my sister doesn't. She may need my help when I can't give it. But our relationships are based upon love, and with that as the constant, we can weather anything.

6. Meet my family's needs—no questions asked. I try to do what I can without expecting something in return.

7. Include my family in my life. My family cannot read my mind any more than I can read theirs. If I need something, I must speak up. Our life-styles are dissimilar, so it is harder for them to perceive what I might need unless I verbalize it. When I live with unexpressed expectations, I sometimes get frustrated and angry. I have learned to avoid such feelings by inviting my family into my heart as well as into my home.

8. Treat others as family. Friends and their children, extended families, ward members, and neighbors can be just like family. I adopt others. It is a marvel to me how my own ability to love and accept others grows as I invite other people into my life.

I send valentines, take friends and children to events, have my cousins stay overnight. It is good for me to vary my schedule, and it is good for them to learn what I can teach.

I Believe

Sometimes being single is like having emotional hiccups. It's uncomfortable and a little embarrassing. I feel these hiccups coming on whenever I don't have anyone to invite to an important social function or when the women at work discuss their children or when I am left off party lists because I don't have a marriage partner. I never like these moments, but on my odyssey through mortality I have found much more contentment in living the gospel and in nurturing my relationship with the Savior than I have found distress from emotional hiccups.

I love life in large measure because my journey through it has forced me to plumb my own depths. My odyssey has been an eventful one in many ways. It has not been all I imagined—for good or ill. It has led me ceaselessly to reverberate with testimony of the gospel.

Two years ago on a trip to Israel with my dear parents, I waded through the cold April water of Hezekiah's tunnel. We came out of the tunnel to see the pool of Siloam, stagnant, filled with algae and garbage. Local hawkers thrust souvenirs in our faces as we shivered in the dusk air, wet well above the knees. Chilled by the wind, I warmly recalled one of the most meaningful passages of scripture to me, the story of the man who was born blind. Perhaps the water was cleaner, perhaps it was not, on the miraculous day that a blind man met the Savior of the world at or near the spot where I stood.

A solitary figure, this blind beggar heard a stranger's voice say, "As long as I am in the world, I am the light of the world." (John 9:5.) What must a man who had never seen light have thought to hear those words?

The Savior anointed the man's eyes and bade him wash in the pool of Siloam. Obediently he washed and "came seeing." (V. 7.) I cannot imagine his joy. But his neighbors did not rejoice with him. Rather, they took him to the Pharisees, who, after repeated questioning and badgering, "reviled him" and "cast him out." (Vv. 28, 34.) He was alone again.

"Jesus heard that they had cast him out; and when he had found him, he said unto him, Dost thou believe on the Son of God?

"He answered and said, Who is he, Lord, that I might believe on him?

"And Jesus said unto him, Thou hast both seen him, and it is he that talketh with thee.

"And he said, Lord, I believe. And he worshipped him." (Vv. 35–38.)

Like the man born blind, I too have moments when I feel reviled and cast out. On my journey through life I am tried and wrenched by both that which does and that which does not happen. And like my fellow traveler, this man born blind who came seeing, I reach towards the light. With him, I look clearly heavenward and state, "Lord, I believe."

With all my heart I choose to live my life, to rush into the surf and get a mouthful of the sweet or the bitter, to make my journey one of love and compassion and poise.

Once my niece Allison was angry at her mother for not giving her what she wanted when she wanted it. Frustrated, she stomped her foot, wiped her tears, and exclaimed, "But a person needs a treat!" How true—every person needs a treat. Happily, I have discovered that marriage, which I believe will one day be part of my joy, is not the treat. The real treat is life itself.

Recognizing God's Will

Ann Laemmlen

Not long ago, I spent several hours in the Lagos, Nigeria, airport waiting for a flight. As I waited, flights came in and flights went out. I watched a variety of people, wondering who they were, where they were coming from, and where they were going. As I watched, I noticed something very interesting happening. Not far from where I was seated, an electrical sidewalk began moving. I was fascinated to watch people approach this powered walkway. It was something unfamiliar to many of the people traveling there. The most common response to it was simply not to take it. Instead, people laden with awkward bags and heavy parcels trudged along beside the automated sidewalk. No big signboard at the beginning advertised this to be an easy or more comfortable way to get to the other end. No fee was collected; no size, age, or weight limit was set. Everyone was welcome. The powered walkway moved silently on, helping those who allowed it to help. Eventually everyone reached the other end.

Ann Laemmlen is an editor for the international magazines of the Church. She graduated with her bachelor of science degree in child development and family relations from Brigham Young University. She became assistant director and then director of an international program for children in Nigeria. The author of three children's books on the Articles of Faith, she has served in ward and stake leadership positions in Relief Society and Sunday School, including nearly a year as Relief Society president in the Eket Nigeria Branch.

As I watched this happening, I wondered what it is in our human nature that tries to insist we can do it ourselves. We want to be in control. We want to be independent. We want to be the decision maker.

As with the people I observed in the airport, I have a choice to make that will greatly affect my travels through life. I can choose to take my journey alone, or I can choose to allow a greater power to help me—a power that will lift and lighten my burdens and make the trip much more enjoyable.

When I was nineteen years old, I decided to go on a mission. I started memorizing scriptures and the discussions. I studied and prepared in every possible way. Anxiously I awaited my twenty-first birthday. But when I turned twenty-one and filled out all my mission application papers, the strong positive feelings I'd had changed to doubt and confusion. I could not understand why. I had prayed and received a positive confirmation about serving a mission. I knew I was to go, but when I prayed and tried to prepare, I felt only distant feelings of confusion. I waited for a flash of inspiration to clue me in to what was happening. When that didn't come, I decided to choose a day, and I told Heavenly Father that if I didn't know what I was to do by that day, he could tell me.

I was on my way home from a semester in Israel via England at that time, and so I planned to spend a day at the London Temple grounds. Once there, I found a quiet and secluded spot under an old oak tree, and there I sat, waiting for an answer to come. It was a long day. I prayed and pondered, and I waited and waited. When the time finally came to go, I was still without a specific answer about my future, but I did feel a certain peace and a feeling that it was all right not to know.

As the months went by, I learned some things I needed to know before I was called to serve in the South Africa Mission eighteen months later. One of the things was learning that a change from "my will" to "thy will" needed to be made in my life.

President Ezra Taft Benson counseled: "Men and women who turn their lives over to God will find out that he can make a lot more out of their lives than they can. He will deepen their joys, expand their vision, quicken their minds, strengthen their muscles, lift their spirits, multiply their blessings, increase their opportunities, comfort their souls, raise up friends, and pour out peace. Whoever will lose his life to God will find he has eternal life." ("Jesus Christ—Gifts and Expectations," *New Era*, May 1975, p. 20.)

Turning my life over to God becomes a challenge for me with the realization that I cannot see the end from the beginning, as our Father in Heaven can. That means it is impossible for me always to set the right goals in the right order. Not only am I not always able to set the right goals without his assistance, but oftentimes I have no idea that a particular option even exists. It will be tragic if I am so busy accomplishing my goals in life that I miss unexpected opportunities that would have come my way had I sought his desires for me instead of my own.

I have always envied people who can sit down and plan things and then make those things happen in their lives. They know what they want to study in school, and they study it. They know what they want to do after school, and they do it. They decide when they want to get married, and they get married. They want to raise a family and have the security of a home, and it happens. And it all looks so simple.

It is really hard for me sometimes because I want those same things and I would love to have that kind of control in my life, but my life just isn't happening that way. I have come to the conclusion that there must be some lessons I need to learn before those things can happen. It's possible that those lessons can be learned only if I relinquish control.

It has been a great exercise of my faith not always to know what will happen next in my life. Making the decision to put my life in His control doesn't always make it easy—but it does always make it right. Still, it's hard to answer others' questions about a future I'm not sure of. It's hard to walk to the edge of the light, and perhaps from time to time, take a step into the darkness. I have learned to identify with the supplication voiced in one of our hymns:

> Lead, kindly Light, amid th' encircling gloom;
> Lead thou me on! . . .
> Keep thou my feet; I do not ask to see
> The distant scene—one step enough for me.

(*Hymns of The Church of Jesus Christ of Latter-day Saints*, 1985, no. 97.)

President Spencer W. Kimball was a man who had absolute trust in the Lord. He had faith to act even when he could not see the end from the beginning. In a tribute to him after his passing, Elder Neal A. Maxwell wrote: "President Kimball's deep trust of the Lord permitted him to do what needed to be done at the front end of a task without becoming too uneasy once the direction was set and the decision was made. He knew enough to follow the counsel of President Harold B. Lee: 'Walk to the edge of the light.' . . .

" . . . he did not take counsel from his fears. He did not wait until everything was perfectly in order before acting. His trust included trust. If one tried to solve in advance all the problems which might occur later, he might never start! The capacity to trust the Lord for *continuous revelation* as to what would later need to be done was clearly a part of the makeup of this very special man." ("Spencer, the Beloved Leader-Servant," *Ensign*, Dec. 1985, pp. 16–17.)

I have often thought how easy life might seem if I could know the end from the beginning—to know how God would have me order and execute my life's plans. Often I have wished I could enter my social security number into a machine and get a computer printout telling me exactly what to do when, where, with whom, and for how long. Perhaps that is what I expected my patriarchal blessing to do for me. I was disappointed when the answers didn't come so easily. Instead, I received blessings I didn't even recognize at the time. For example, I was promised my faith would be strengthened through a variety of important experiences. Well, that was fine and good, but I wanted to know then what those experiences were! I wanted to know if I was supposed to go on a mission. I wanted to know what I should study in school and what my career options would be. I wanted to know if I'd get married, when, and to whom. Instead, I was instructed to keep my trust in the giver of all my gifts and blessings, seek him humbly and diligently, listen to the sweet and peaceful whisperings of the still small voice, and then my duties would be made plain. I was frustrated that my path wasn't made crystal clear. I wanted all the answers, and I wanted them now!

I have since learned a very important lesson. When I would pray and pray to know what to do next in my life, the answer always seemed to come, again and again, that my duties would be made plain. That was reassuring, but it didn't answer my questions. I wanted to know specifically what those duties were. Through all of this I have learned that God is not a distributor of answers. He is a creator of situations leading to the exaltation of his children. As I work with this process, I am becoming a better person, and I am learning to develop absolute trust in the Lord.

As I try hard to exercise this kind of trust, I find that God is making much more of my life than I would or could. I probably would have stuck to the traditional expectations of going to school, finding a husband, getting married, and having babies. Instead of having this kind of life-style, I have been led to peoples, countries, and opportunities I never even knew existed. I have had to stretch and grow in ways I never would have known to be possible. I have made friends who add great variety and blessings to my life.

I have recently concluded three years of living and working in Nigeria, West Africa, on a child health project. I hadn't planned to go back to Africa after my mission. It wasn't a goal I set and worked for as my mission had been. It was a totally unexpected opportunity.

Before I knew I would be returning to Africa, I decided that if I was willing and my life was flexible, there would be opportunities to serve. I had seen that those who want to serve, do serve. So instead of planning a lot of specific things I wanted to do, I tried to prepare my heart. I prayed hard for a willing attitude and a desire to serve. I prayed for opportunities to help somewhere, somehow, and I tried hard to be prepared and available to help wherever I could.

When the invitation to return to Africa was extended to me, it was easy to recognize that I had been prepared to accept it, even though it was not what I was expecting. At that time, I was preparing for graduation from Brigham Young University, and I had some ideas for my future. I was also twenty-five years old, and stepping out of circulation for three years was not something I was considering. Then one evening, when I was on my way home from school and work, I stopped to pick up my mail. In it was a magazine with a feature story on the weather patterns that were creating havoc all over the globe. I looked at page after page of destruction and desperation. As I turned to photographs of children on the African continent, my heart could no longer contain all I was feeling. I sat down and wept.

I did not sleep much that night. Some things happened in my heart that I don't know how to explain. Promises were made, and commitments were renewed. The very next day I was asked to go to Nigeria. I knew I had been prepared, and I knew I must go.

It had taken me a long time to be able to tell Heavenly Father honestly that I would do whatever he asked me to do. Once I decided to turn my life over to God, as President Benson counseled, I hoped the rest would be easy. It hasn't been. I also hoped that the will of God wouldn't be too far from my own. But his expectations are different from mine—his are much higher. The fulfilling of those expectations often comes in unexpected ways.

Finding out what God wants me to do has been my biggest challenge, and for me, this step takes a lot of energy. I have found it helpful, as I make plans and prepare for my life's activities, to list and consider all conceivable options, setting no limitations. This list includes things I want to learn, places I want to go, people I want to spend time with, books I want to read, subjects I want to study, work I want to do, and spiritual qualities I want to develop. I have a special book where I keep these things recorded. I call it my plan book.

I try hard to keep myself familiar with these thoughts, ideas, and plans, and I add to them and make changes as time goes by. It has been helpful to refer to my patriarchal blessing, taking special note of blessings, gifts, and admonitions. This gives me some clue to my Father's expectations for me. Because he sets no limits, I try not to. And I am learning how blessed I am to have so many choices.

Recently, while in Nigeria, I learned a great lesson about the blessing of free agency when I was asked to teach a Relief Society lesson on decision-making. I asked my Nigerian sisters about the choices they have to make each day. As soon as I asked the question and saw their blank faces, I realized how my life had been blessed with agency in ways their lives had not. I could understand why they were unable to respond to my question when I thought about what kinds of activities fill their days. With mouths to feed and farming to do and crops to grow and water to carry and firewood to collect and mud homes to keep clean and food to find and sick children to care for and distances to walk and burdens to carry—virtually no time, energy, or opportunity for choices remained.

These sisters don't get to choose what clothing to put on each morning, which brand of foods to feed their children, what books to read, what service organization to join, what classes to enroll in, where to go on their next vacation, what video to check out, how to invest their savings, which coupons to clip, and which stores to shop in. Many of them didn't even have the choice about what they wanted to do when they grew up or who they would marry. Survival, circumstance, and tradition determine their life's activities. Their agency has limitations mine doesn't have. Choices are blessings. The more choices I have, the more freedom I have.

When I make plans for my life's activities, of what use is agency if I fail to exercise it? The more options I give myself, the more doors I open, the greater my freedom to choose. I know many people limited by circumstances beyond their control who would love dearly to have the choices I do. I value my freedom to choose, my freedom to become.

In seeking to know what God would have me do, I must consider every option. I can limit my freedom to become by setting narrow or rigid goals or by insisting God meet certain conditions with which I can comfortably comply. Or I can expand my freedom by considering all my choices and then bending my will to his in the decision making.

Three of the most helpful commandments I have found to assist me in the discovery of God's will are daily prayer, daily scripture study, and journal writing. Keeping these commandments helps me remember that God did not send me to this earth to flounder and perhaps, by chance, to discover some of the things I was sent here to learn. He is close to me, and he will intervene in my life and on my behalf as much as I will allow him. He wants me to trust in him and seek his counsel. Obeying all three of these commandments strengthens and enhances my ability to communicate with him. Revelation is communication. Receiving continuous personal revelation is necessary and essential to my discovering what God would have me do from day to day and year to year.

In prayer I can present my ideas to God in a spirit that is receptive to feelings of warmth, peace, and calm, or I may feel hesitancy, frustration, and stupor. He has instructed us to "study it out in your mind; then you must ask me if it be right, and if it is right, . . . your bosom shall burn within you; therefore, you shall feel that it is right. But if it be not right you shall have no such feelings, but you shall have a stupor of thought that shall cause you to forget the thing which is wrong." (D&C 9:8–9.) Responses to my prayers usually come as feelings and impressions rather than as clear-cut, well-defined answers or instructions of where to go or what to do. It is my responsibility to make those decisions before going to the Lord in prayer. He will confirm my decision or let me know that I need to make a different decision to present to him. That is what I experienced when I was preparing to go on my mission.

President N. Eldon Tanner taught me a very important lesson when once, in essence, he said, "If in doubt, don't do it." To me that means unless I have received an assurance from Heavenly Father that what I am planning to do is in complete accordance with his will, I should not proceed. Rather, I should repeat the process as many times as necessary until I discover what he would have me do. He will not forsake me, but he will temper and refine me. And when, at last, the discovery is made, he will bless me with an unmistakable assurance that I have found it.

It seems that my ability to recognize God's will increases in direct proportion to my familiarity with his words. When I want to speak to God I pray. When I want him to speak to me, I listen in prayer and read the scriptures. Daily contact with the inspired words in the scriptures keeps my mind familiar with God's ways. The more familiar I am with his thoughts and feelings, the more like his my own become.

Through scripture study I can also learn how generations of men and women traveled varied paths to their eternal rewards. By studying their lives, I can shape my own after the ones who traveled where I want to go. For example, it is helpful to me to read about the brother of Jared and how the Lord responded to his questions and tutored him in such a way that faith and trust led to a perfect knowledge of God and of all things. (See Ether 2–3.)

The Lord had particular things in mind for the brother of Jared and his family. The Lord could see the land of promise that lay ahead. The brother of Jared could not. The scriptures tell us that the Lord would not suffer that they should stop at a certain place but that they should continue even unto the land of promise, which was choice above all other lands. (See Ether 2:7.) As I read how the Lord instructed the brother of Jared step by step, I can imagine some of the feelings that may have gone through his heart. There have been times in my life when I felt as if I were being asked to step into a barge without light, headed for a place I did not know. It's frightening. But the Lord has helped me and prepared me in much the same way he helped the brother of Jared. I know that the Lord will not suffer that I should stop at certain places but that I should continue instead to the places he has in mind for me.

The commandment to keep a journal is as important to me as prayer and scripture study because through writing in my journal, I receive communication from my Heavenly Father. The Spirit speaks to our hearts and minds. As I write, I find there may already be lessons and answers inside me, waiting to be recognized. I also find it extremely helpful to be able to empty my thoughts and clear the clutter that builds up in my mind. It takes a lot of mental energy to hang on to everything I want to remember. I'd rather use that energy generating new thoughts and ideas. When my mind is uncluttered, it is easier to recognize and respond to the promptings of the Spirit.

It has been fascinating to me to skim back through years of journal entries and see the mountains and valleys I've climbed and the plateaus I've rested upon. I am reminded of months of searching for direction and insight and then the sudden joy of discovery in an unexpected moment, usually in an unexpected way. I can see how my prayers have been answered in a variety of ways: through people and relationships, through travel and experience, through study and discovery. As I see how one thing in my life has led me to the next, my ability to trust has been strengthened and the anxiety I sometimes feel about what should come next in my life dissipates.

After I have discovered what God would have me do, the next step is obvious: I do it! Unless, of course, I change my mind and tell Heavenly Father he may have made a mistake. After all, everyone knows we have been commanded to multiply and replenish the earth, and certainly the place for me to do that is not in a remote village in the dark of Africa. Or, "Okay, okay, I'll go on a mission. Just make sure it's foreign and exotic—I need to learn a foreign language so I can pass those university language requirements when I get home."

It must be rather amusing at times, when Heavenly Father listens to my responses to his responses. Maybe sometimes the reason he seems to take so long answering my petitions is that he knows I don't really want to hear what he has to say. It takes courage for me to say yes when it's the right thing to do, just as it takes courage to say no when something is not right. Often it's not until I am in a position to look back on my life that I can see reasons and patterns and gain perspectives that may have been hidden from my view at the time certain paths were unfolded and decisions made. Again, I must trust in the master planner, and remember the position from which his perspective comes.

So, with that trust, I do it. I take the risk, I make the sacrifice. I stretch, I learn, I grow, and I begin to experience true joy and happiness. I find, as President Benson promised, that my joys deepen, my vision expands, my mind is quickened, my muscles are strengthened, my spirits are lifted, my blessings are multiplied, my opportunities are increased, my soul receives comfort, friends are raised up, and my life is filled with peace. I believe that is what it means to fill the full measure of my creation. That is the optimal life I can experience, no matter who I am, no matter what my circumstances may be. If I have that sweet assurance that I am where I am supposed to be, doing what I am supposed to be doing, I feel confident, and I relax and enjoy life because I know that God will not, cannot, withhold blessings from me when I am doing what he has asked me to do.

Sometimes it happens that as I am going along my merry way, doing what I know is right for me, I notice that the people around me are doing something different. Sometimes I begin to wonder why I'm not doing the same things they are doing. I begin to wonder if maybe I have made a mistake. Sometimes the novelty of doing something different wears off after a few months, and I find myself wondering what I've gotten myself into. I see friends doing things I expected or planned I would be doing, and I am not doing those things yet in my own life.

I sometimes wonder if I ever will. Sometimes it seems as if everyone else is happier than I. When these feelings come into my heart, the peace and calm slip away. I get anxious or discouraged or restless. When I feel a need to worry about what I am doing with my life, I try to find out why. Maybe it's time for a change. Maybe it's time to make some new decisions. Maybe Heavenly Father is telling me I'm getting too comfortable and complacent with my life, and it's time for some new lessons. Heavenly Father is teaching me to feel these things when it is time to change. If I allow him, he will gently nudge me in the direction I need to go.

Sometimes I feel doubts even when I am doing the right things. The struggle between "my will" and "thy will" often continues even after decisions have been made. When this happens, I seek reassurance that the things I am doing are the right things. When Oliver Cowdery later questioned a divine manifestation he had received concerning the truthfulness of the Book of Mormon, the Lord said to him, "If you desire a further witness, cast your mind upon the night that you cried unto me in your heart, that you might know concerning the truth of these things. Did I not speak peace to your mind concerning the matter? What greater witness can you have than from God?" (D&C 6:22–23.)

Oliver Cowdery needed to be reminded of the answer he had received earlier. Heavenly Father will either reconfirm something he has already told me, or he will help me find out what I should be doing differently. So I go from there and seek that assurance, and then I can move forward again with confidence.

I am grateful to have a Father in Heaven who loves me enough to promise that if I trust in him with all my heart and lean not unto my own understanding but in all my ways acknowledge him, he will direct my paths. (See Proverbs 3:5–6.) The choice is mine. I can choose to do it myself, or I can allow a greater power to help me—a power that will lift and lighten my burdens and make the trip much more enjoyable.

My goals in life have changed considerably since I made the decision to seek God's will and then do it. Often I can imagine easier, more comfortable things to do, but when I'm doing what I know is right, I cannot imagine feeling greater peace and happiness. It's no one's responsibility but my own to find that peace, and by so doing, prepare for my eternal reward, for "he who doeth the works of righteousness shall receive his reward, even peace in this world, and eternal life in the world to come." (D&C 59:23.)

Person in Process

Elizabeth A. Shaw

Single is my natural state. I was born single. I grew up single. I was baptized single, and I went through the temple single. I went to college and got a job single. I pray single, shop single, and think single. Single is easy.

To be married would be the aberration—suddenly living with a stranger, eating strange food, picking up strange socks, producing and living with more strange people, and never again knowing that when the phone rings, it rings just for you.

I am aware that defending the single state is risky business—precisely because it's seen as just that, a defense. But even in my mid thirties I am willing to look my skeptics in the eye and declare staunchly: Single has been fun.

There are reasons for saying that. I have considered the relative advantages of the single and the married states, and I have concluded that singleness has more than selfish benefits. Contrary to the persistent myth, Mormon female singleness is not

Elizabeth A. Shaw is an attorney practicing in Los Angeles, California. She earned her bachelor of arts and master of arts degrees in English from Brigham Young University and her juris doctor degree from the University of Utah College of Law. Before becoming an attorney, she was an editor for the Ensign *and for Brigham Young University Press. Her Church service has included a number of leadership and teaching positions in Relief Society and Sunday School and several years on general Church writing committees.*

the equivalent of ugly, lonely, dull, and despairing. Those adjectives apply just as accurately—or inaccurately—to Mormon female married. On the contrary, I have found being single to be a productive, stretching, confidence-building condition, just as marriage can be. Single or married, I can be happy or unhappy, love intensely, receive intense love, learn unselfishness, develop and express talents, and come to know the Lord.

I don't believe my experiences or conclusions as a single Mormon woman are atypical. But I do not believe we talk enough to the Church at large—or to each other—about those feelings and experiences. As a result, I think we may sometimes forget how "normal" we all really are. I am thus willing to risk some personal exposure in this essay, in the hope that it may prompt other sharing.

I was born and raised in Wyoming in an active Mormon family, even though my parents divorced when I was fourteen. I went to Brigham Young University for bachelor's and master's degrees in English, spent five years as a book and magazine editor, and then, like a good many others hitting thirty, reevaluated my career objectives and went to law school. I have been practicing law in Los Angeles for the past four years. With some occasional exceptions, I have not been bored. I can divide my primary sources of joy and growth since going off to college into three categories: career, people, and the Lord.

For me, at least, the importance of a satisfying career cannot be overemphasized. I spend more time in my career than in any other activity, give it more thought, and deal there with more anxieties. It had better be right. But even "right" can be a compromise. While my first desire for all my waking moments, if I lived in some never-never land, might be to sit under a tree with orange juice and barbecued potato chips reading John Fowles novels, I have made concessions to reality. I acknowledge the necessity of gainful employment. But I have tried not to lose sight of what it is I really love to do, and that has made all the difference.

That was not an automatic insight. I went to Brigham Young University as a declared home economics major, convinced in my teenage zeal to be perfect that that was The One True Major at The Lord's University. It took almost a year before I really believed that being a good Mormon girl and majoring in English were not incompatible. I still remember the joy of that decision.

Although I didn't find English an easy major, it fed my soul. I remember exquisite excitement reading Wordsworth's *Prelude* and Keats's *Endymion* for Marion Brady's Romantic Lit class. I remember the intense satisfaction of finally understanding a Wallace Stevens poem, after considerable struggle. I remember tangible glee at spying a solitary corner of the library, treasuring the knowledge that I had two uninterrupted hours to read *Twelfth Night*. And I remember the feeling I had as a college senior, studying in my hot little upstairs bedroom, that life and knowledge and God were all coming together and that my head and heart would burst with the sheer delight of wrapping myself in new and old truth.

Graduate school was better yet. In my second year as a teacher of freshman composition, I discovered that I really liked teaching. It gave me confidence with language and people, both in and out of books. The thesis period was grueling, the orals an ordeal, but I hated to leave the (mentally) ivied halls of academia when it was all over.

In the next stage of my career saga I felt one of the first—and most powerful—messages from the Lord regarding my career. Up to this point I had mainly just been following my inclinations. The message was not so much that the Lord had a specific career in mind for me, but that he wanted me to be happy and would help me to be so. This little miracle occurred in San Francisco.

After graduate school, a good friend and I loaded up our two Plymouths and set off across the desert to The City. We were sure we would easily find jobs teaching in one of the many Bay Area junior colleges. Alas, we spent a year as secretaries instead. It was the mid seventies, and there was a humanities glut. I loved the people where I worked, the Stanford Ward, and the northern California weather, but I was utterly miserable in my job. I mailed off reams of resumes and even interviewed with the CIA (a gruff, Lee Marvin-type character in a cavernous marble room, downtown in the Federal Building). But for the first time something I wanted intensely—a satisfying job—seemed utterly out of my control.

I turned with some desperation to the Lord. I fasted and prayed intently, with an almost naive faith that he would help. I remember well the day that he did, unmistakably and unequivocally. I felt strongly prompted to send my resume and go interview at a place I had not thought of before. It was an eerie feeling, applying for a job that the Lord had found for me. A month later I was a scholarly books editor at BYU Press.

I consider that job a gift. I hauled a little carpet into my dark, interior office and relished going in on Saturdays. The job involved much more than manuscripts: I hung out around the pressmen and made friends with the "strippers" and graphic artists, soaking in the whole publishing process. It was hard to leave when, two years later, family responsibilities required that I move to Salt Lake City. When I moved, I went to work as an editor in the LDS Church curriculum editing department and then at the *Ensign* magazine. All along, I was tutored and inspired by colleagues and exhilarated by the processes of clarity and expression.

I had just started my third year with the *Ensign* when I was assigned to a project that involved researching legal issues and interviewing Rex Lee, then dean of the BYU law school. It dawned on me that law was language, and I knew I wanted to go to law school. My encouragement from the Lord at this next step was not as specific as the guidance into editing had been. Still, after prayer, I felt peaceful about the decision and felt his assistance in the application and acceptance process.

The transition from warm Church Office Building womb into the University of Utah law school battleground was initially traumatic. I wasn't thrilled by the occasional public humiliation of the law school class, and I discovered that I wasn't as relentlessly competitive as some of my younger classmates. But my writing experience was a decided asset: in my second year I made Law Review. As a third-year law student I taught legal research and writing to freshman law students, a happy combination of several of my favorite pastimes. By graduation, law school had become the womb, and I indulged nostalgic feelings at leaving.

I had accepted a job with a Los Angeles law firm and so drove off into the sunset in my U-Haul truck right after the ceremonies. I found an apartment in yuppie Brentwood and hunkered down to the worst summer of my life, studying for the California bar exam. California has the lowest pass rate of any state (less than 50 percent), and even such top-rated law schools as Stanford claim only 70 percent first-time success. After studying eight to ten hours a day for two months, I came home exhausted and depressed on the second day of the three-day exam. I was sure I had failed. I hadn't been home long when my mother called from Utah to say, "The Lord has told me you have passed." I still had one day of the exam to go, but I knew if my mother said the Lord had said so, it was so. I went back to the exam the next day confident and calm and secretly elated. Another serendipitous gift from God in my career.

I haven't loved law every minute, but I do love the discipline and precision and complexity of it. And I like the relative economic freedom it has given me, although at the cost of some free time. By and large, I also like the people it has put me with. Intelligent, considering, energetic people have been my models and friends.

In looking back over approximately fifteen years of career, including graduate school, I do see a curious interplay of my own desires and proclivities on the one hand and the Lord's assistance and reassurance on the other. The important conclusion, for me, is that I did not feel alone at key moments. In real and sometimes even dramatic ways, I have been aware that success and happiness in my chosen career were not irrelevant to the Lord.

A second source of knowledge and fulfillment for me has been people: discovering and loving my family, my friends, and myself. One of the great joys of my extended single state has been the time and opportunity to develop an amazing friendship with my mother. Even from a thousand miles' distance, we share books, recipes, and delight with a new dress. We can talk each other out of depression and pray each other out of crises. Moments of petty irritation still surface occasionally, but each of us knows she is the other's best friend, safe harbor, and ready assistant. There has been unspeakable joy for me in that knowledge. One of my rare moments of panic about my singleness came with the realization one day that my mother would someday die. When she did, there would be no one on earth who loved me and accepted me absolutely. Only then did I realize what a great thing it is to be so loved.

Other friends have also shaped and sustained me: Sharon Miller Banks, whose gentle humor shamed me out of sophomoric moodiness; my cousin Susan Stevens Tuft, with whom I read the Bible, prayed, and learned that two people could be totally honest with each other, even on painful topics, and love more because of it; Linda Madsen Sheffield, who introduced me to art and the beauty of a disciplined life; Susan Rich Nelson, whose total dedication to the Church and ability to sacrifice and obey and give amaze me still; Gigi Doty, for whom math and Bach were twin passions and who seemed to me to be utterly and enviably free of the burden of public opinion; Linda Stahle Cooper,who shared with me the joy of reading C. S. Lewis. With them I have delighted in the processes of life, gathering energy from self-awareness and change.

More recently important are those friends who have remained single with me. These have been energetic and competent women such as Kathleen Lubeck and Janet Sant. With them I have shared the joy and pain of good and not-so-good romance, of coming to an adult relationship with the Church, of maturing in faith, and of exploring the ways of God. With them and others I have discussed loneliness and largely kept it at bay because of the relief of full expression on a given subject and the return compliment of understanding. I am convinced that inarticulateness and loneliness are causes and effects of each other. I can't discuss everything that is vital to me with each of my friends, but I am blessed with the wonderful phenomenon of honest communication with a variety of understanding friends on the subjects that are important to me.

With some small surprise, I have discovered that a single person can be very close to a married couple. Shortly after moving to Los Angeles I renewed acquaintance with an old BYU friend, D'Ann Allred, now married to Robert Stoddard. Being somewhat cynical and otherwise worn-out after law school and the bar exam, I was impressed with the way these two intelligent, creative, and aware people had wholeheartedly given themselves to the Lord, with the consequence that miracles seemed to occur regularly in their lives. I respected their humility and integrity and, largely because of the promise their lives represented, set about to try to understand and develop faith.

Robert and D'Ann carried their (slightly burned) goose over to my apartment for Christmas dinner, I read Chekhov with Robert as he finished his master's thesis, and we talked about God and change. Largely because of Robert and D'Ann's experiences, I too finally went to a Latter-day Saint psychologist I trusted and there I talked, cried, faced the unmasked me, and decided I could live with her. The Lord was there, too, directly, as he has been in other key friendships during these past two years.

Reaching for the Lord has been a third source of joy and growth for me, in addition to career and people. I have always been very involved in Church activities, and basic Church doctrines have always seemed logical and natural to me. Beginning about the time I went to graduate school, however, I became aware that the world—including the Church—wasn't pure and simple. Motives of Church leaders whom I had naively deified seemed to me to be sometimes political, their actions occasionally unjust.

I was concerned about the status of women, first in the Church, and then with the Lord. For awhile I avoided general conferences, as the speeches there seemed to me to be especially condescending and trivial. It was an effort to go to Relief Society; it seemed to me to be unnecessary, the discussions there insincere and obvious. I believed in God, I believed Joseph Smith had seen a vision and restored the Church, I prayed and fasted and tried to keep my personal life congruent with my beliefs, I held Church jobs. But I believed Church programs to be in need of reform, and Church leaders in need of humility and repentance. I went to sacrament meeting but preferred to read by myself on the back row when I found the speakers boring (which was more often than not).

Fortunately, during this period I had several good bishops and other Church leaders I could talk to frankly: Gordon Madsen, my uncle Bill Partridge, Leo Jardine, Bert Scoll, Bob Rees, and the Stoddards. I found that my concerns were not invalid, that others had seen and still believed. I read *Dialogue* and the *Ensign*. I listened to speakers at *Sunstone* symposia and tried general conference again. I learned that others had worked through their doubts and fused faith and integrity. Eugene England's *Dialogues with Myself*, Lavina Fielding Anderson's "On Being Happy: An Exercise in Spiritual Autobiography" (*Exponent II*, Summer 1982), Bruce Hafen, Dean Larson, Paul Toscano, Lynn Scoresby, Neal Maxwell, Spencer W. Kimball, C. S. Lewis, Alma and King Benjamin, Scott Peck, Hugh Nibley, Carlfred Broderick: these were my spiritual mentors. I read, underlined, reread. I found I did believe in faith and charity. I found I wanted them both.

Especially important to me in the process of maturing my faith and acceptance has been the temple. I love the symbolism there, the open-endedness and ambiguity. I love the purity and the strong feeling I often have there that I am at what Hugh Nibley calls an intersection between heaven and earth. On one occasion, shortly after I entered law school, when I had been seriously troubled for several weeks about my status and potential as a woman, I went to the temple fasting and praying for reassurance. I was finding troublesome signals in scripture, from the pulpit, and even in the temple itself that women were deemed less capable than men of thinking, of making decisions, of bearing responsibility, of creating more than just biologically. I felt that I could understand and excuse such attitudes in men, but I was beginning to feel that perhaps I really was a lesser creature than a man in the Lord's eyes as well. I could not understand why the Lord would do that to me. I felt betrayed and pained, and I took it up with him in the temple.

Near the end of the session he responded, directly and powerfully, in a kind of vision sense. Since then I have known that even though there may be injustices on earth, women—no, it was even more specific to me—were every bit the equal of men in capability and power, and women—I—could and would receive glory and joy beyond my wildest imaginings, and things would be made right. I felt God's specific love and perspective for an intense, golden instant. I go to the temple with awe and expectation, and I am rarely disappointed.

I have found prayer to be another vital phenomenon. When I take the time and make an honest, strong effort to humble myself, there has come the wonder of actual dialogue, with a real person on the other end. The sense of God that this brings inevitably colors my optimism and my willingness to serve. It is power in itself.

And I confess that I am beginning to learn, though sometimes painfully, the metaphysics of Church service. I believe it is, quite simply, essential. It is a unique forum for human interaction, one where, if you give yourself wholeheartedly, you inevitably see the hand of God exposed and learn, through sacrifice, unselfish love. There are enormous frustrations in Church service as well. I am not yet to the point where I accept each Church calling with joy. But I do accept with faith.

In short, I do not believe for an instant that I have been denied the lessons of life because I am single. It is precisely because I am single that I have learned some of those lessons. I even believe that my singleness is in some unfathomable way according to design. I believe that I have been blessed to be single, for perhaps a number of larger purposes. I don't know all those purposes, but I have felt the Lord sharing my life, and that is peace and joy.

"DO Something, Madam . . ."

Margot J. Butler

It is somewhat difficult for me to write this as a "single person," primarily because I think of myself as a "person." "Single" is one of the adjectives that could describe my life-style, but it is only one, and it is not a focal point. Some people like to blame their problems and unhappiness on other people or on facets of their lives—like being single, overweight, deaf. I don't believe in that. I believe we are children of God with personalities that interact with possibilities. Out of this interaction, I make my life. I make it whether I am single or married, overweight or underweight, deaf or hearing, black or white. Perhaps by being single I am more visible in that when I do something, it is identified with me, the individual, not as so-and-so's wife or so-and-so's mother. Had I married, I would have had different opportunities and different situations in which to function, but the personality that I brought with me would probably have

---

Margot J. Butler is a coordinator of special education in Salt Lake City for the Church Educational System. Her wide-ranging teaching experience has taken her from her birthplace in Melbourne, Australia, to such diverse places as Frankfurt, Germany, and Gooding, Idaho, where she taught in the Idaho School for the Deaf. Her work with special education, including service as the curriculum coordinator for the Utah School for the Deaf, earned her the Golden Key Award from the governor of Utah. Her Church service has included callings to the general board of the Young Women's Mutual Improvement Association and to writing committees for Church curriculum.

made much the same decisions and responded much the same in either married or single blessedness.

Consider my life as the ward chorister. That is one of the great callings of the Church. One gets to choose the hymns! One gets to set the mood for the meeting and even shorten it if some well-meaning but long-winded speaker goes overtime.

Many are the meetings where as ward chorister I became a little nervous as the minute hand circled closer and closer to the closing hour and the speaker was still going strong. (If speakers can't handle time here, just think what sacrament meeting is going to be like in eternity!) As the meeting went longer, I would take out the hymnbook and decide, in the interest of other meetings and the roast at home in the oven, which verse I would leave out. As the speaker went longer, and verses were honed down to one, I sometimes switched to the short doxology to finish: "Praise God, from whom all blessings flow. . . . " Would a married person have done any differently?

Later I was called to the stake music committee. Someone had told us there were to be no more stake music committees. That was wonderful because if there were no longer to be such things as stake music committees, we could write our own job descriptions. I immediately went from being the secretary who took minutes and telephoned people to being the executive secretary who did exactly the same thing.

We were to suggest musical numbers that might be appropriate for the choir to sing in stake conference, which that year would fall on Easter. Since the high councilor in charge of the stake music committee was not very musical, whoever suggested a piece would then run over to the piano and play a few bars. Being the executive secretary to a committee that insisted on running to the piano every few minutes and playing a few bars gave me some difficulty in taking minutes. Does one name the piece and then write a few bars?

Finally, Jay Welch, the chairman of our committee, made a suggestion that was accepted by the conference committee. The choir would sing a beautiful chorus from Mascagni's opera, *Cavaliera Rusticana*, because it is set at Easter. That was it. The choir would sing Mascagni. But I was taking the minutes.

"How do you spell *Mascagni*?"

Jay's perfectly straight-faced answer came, "It's spelled like *pizza*, but with different letters."

I laughed more in that job than in any other job I can remember, which is just and proper because "a merry heart doeth good like a medicine." (Proverbs 17:22.) Would I have had more fun—or less—as the stake music committee secretary had I been married?

Those are Church jobs to which I have been called. There are also Church jobs for which I volunteered. Once I visited an unsuspecting stake when I was on the YWMIA General Board. The stake president got up in the leadership meeting and announced that the opening hymn would be dispensed with because the only person who could play the piano was not there. Well, what could I say to that? Of course. I volunteered to play the hymn. I didn't offer to play the hymn well, but I did offer to play it. I figured if someone played the piano better than I did, that someone should have offered first. Because there was no one who played the piano at all, I was pretty safe.

I did the same thing once while vacationing in Mexico. I went to a ward where no one could play the piano. The song leader started a cappella—way too low. A soprano in the congregation started singing in a higher pitch, so both keys were being sung at the same time. It was an experience, to put it mildly.

The next Sunday I thought I would offer to play if a piano player didn't turn up. I looked for someone to volunteer, but as my Spanish does not fall trippingly from my tongue, the meeting started with no piano accompaniment. (It was really an organ, but if you've seen one keyboard, haven't you seen them all?) After a few minutes the brother conducting the meeting asked if anyone could play the piano. Spanish does not fall trippingly upon my ear, either, but some words are international, so I got up to play the organ. The first hymn went okay. After that I sat next to a sister who pointed to the page I was to play when the brother announced it. I couldn't read the Spanish so the words didn't help, but I sight-read the hymn in my mind as I walked to the organ so I could start playing at the right tempo.

One hymn gave me trouble. As I walked to the organ, I went over it in my mind, but it made no sense at all. I should have known the hymn, but I didn't. I would just have to wing it. It was embarrassing to have volunteered and then not to have the foggiest notion what I was going to play, but I sat down and started. By the time I got to the second measure, I had figured out that it was "I Stand All Amazed," with the melody written all in the left hand. Would I have played that music differently with a diamond on my left hand?

Lest you think that I am innately musical, let me hasten to remind you that accepting a job in the Church does not mean that one is necessarily talented. It merely means that when one was called, one said, "Yes." My friend A. Hamer Reiser, who is a doctor, gave me a prescription sheet, dated and legitimately signed—which makes it a legitimate prescription—and it says only, "Say no." But that didn't prevent me from being called as president of the ward Primary. I reminded the bishop that such jobs are usually given to doting mothers who try to smile a lot and make visual aids, not to unmarried schoolteachers who have perfected the evil eye and bestow it upon anyone who misbehaves. We both agreed, though, that we wanted the children in the ward to learn the gospel, so I became president.

Once we invited the stake president and the bishop to come to Primary so that all the children could interview them and get to know them. They were all well-behaved (the children, not the stake president and the bishop, although they were well behaved, too). The children asked the questions they had practiced: "What is your church job?" "What are your hobbies?" and so on, and did very well. It was going beautifully and according to plan. As a parting shot I asked if the children had any more questions they wanted to ask the stake president. One child had a final question. What was his Sabbath-day question to this spiritual leader of the whole stake?

"Where did you buy your TV?"

The stake president was an old pro. He didn't flicker an eyelash. In fact, he acted as if that was the very question he had come to answer that day. He smiled broadly and answered the boy.

We had great sport in Primary. We acted out the whole Old Testament—well, almost the whole Old Testament. When Joshua needed to take Jericho, we held up four blankets in a square to represent the walls. We had Rahab inside the walls because she was the only one from the city with a speaking part. Around the walls marched seven ward members who played, with varying skill, the trumpet. All had their heads swathed in white pillow slips to show that they were priests. Just in case you ever consider doing this yourself, let me tell you that the white pillow slips were almost harder to come by than the trumpeters since florals and patterns have come into fashion.

Anyway, they marched around the walls as prescribed, while I told the story. At the end the children of Israel shouted, so I told the Primary children that they were the children of Israel and they got to shout. Do you know how loud the noise is when eighty Primary children shout at the top of their lungs? Let me tell you, LOUD! If the original children of Israel shouted half as loudly as our Primary children, the walls of Jericho fell down just out of shock. But the adults had fun, and the children had fun. They have even heard of Joshua now, and I hope they continue the friendship their whole lives. What mother in Zion could do more?

Another wonderful maternal job was teaching thirteen-year-old cherubs in Sunday School. I would never suggest that their behavior was cherubic, but they were cherubs, nonetheless, although thirteen-year-old cherubs are in a class all their own. The boys would not sit anywhere near the girls, and with the size of our classroom, that was hard to manage. I tried stopping and being quiet when they were not attentive. I did a lot of stopping and being quiet. The cherubs did not. They neither stopped nor were quiet. It was a test to see who was more interesting, me, or the boys. It was obviously the boys, but one cannot be overcome by the obvious. What was not obvious was that they all wanted to learn. I believe everyone wants to learn, and other behavior is just a cover-up. I persevered. They decided they wanted to learn something. They found that it was even fun to behave like people. They were great. I liked and respected them then, and though the thirteen-year-old behavior is now long gone, the liking and respecting are still there.

I was the president of the Young Women in the Frankfurt Ward in the servicemen's stake in Europe the year I taught school there. When the bishop called me, I told him that I had neither of the two requisites for the job. He looked startled. He was afraid I was going to say I did not have a testimony; not so, I had a testimony. What I did not have was either a car or a telephone. I know that some areas get along fine without them and don't expect them, but this ward was used to transportation and telephone calls. It is fine to be spiritual, but it does not hurt to be prepared for the practical as well. Do you think perhaps I would have had a car and a telephone if I'd had a husband?

One of my present jobs is teaching the Gospel Doctrine class. It is a lot harder to teach than Primary, not because you need to know more, but because it is a lot harder to maintain a level of active exuberance. In Primary the activity level sometimes approached mayhem, but the activity level of the Gospel Doctrine classes can slide into rigor mortis. It is a delight to help keep the adults alive and awake, both married and single.

Of course, I don't learn all my lessons in church. One afternoon I was teaching a class of hearing-impaired students in school. We were all hot and tired—I was hot, and they were tired—and the lesson was coming to a close. I asked a question just to tie the lesson up.

"Who was President of the United States then?"

One of the students thought for a moment and then mumbled, "Hmmmmmmm Hnngn."

I didn't understand him and asked him to repeat his answer, which was as unintelligible to me the second time. His buddy sitting next to him said, "He said, 'Abraham Lincoln.' "

I looked at the boy. "Is that what you said?"

He nodded.

"Say it again." It was still not clear, but I thanked him for his answer and was pleased that he knew.

Later I asked his buddy, "How did you know that was what he said? That did not look (lip reading) like Abraham Lincoln, and it didn't sound like Abraham Lincoln."

He looked at this poor simpleton of a teacher, sighed patiently, and explained, "He's my friend."

Oh, that we all had friends like that. Oh, that we were so in tune with people that we would always understand what they mean. Classes would be better places, and so would every place else.

Now Jack was a different kettle of fish. Jack was twelve years old and a lot smarter than I, and we both knew it. One thing I learned early in teaching was that just because I was older did not mean that I was smarter. Jack was into all the mischief that a twelve-year-old gets into. His being hearing impaired did not seem to slow him down any. If it did, I shudder to think what he could have got into if his hearing had been normal and he had been open to more opportunities.

One day we were discussing the inconvenience of handicapping conditions. I made the mistake of mentioning his hearing loss, so he told me that his hearing loss didn't slow him down very much, and I agreed. "I know that you adjust very well. You compensate magnificently. You are very smart, but you are deaf, so that you don't hear everything, and that is considered a handicap." I thought I had put it well and succinctly.

Jack raised his twelve-year-old eyebrows and told me this story: "There is this wild bull in a field. Around the field is a fence with no place to get through except one very small opening. You and I are in the field. The bull sees us and charges. We run to the opening, and I fit through, but you don't. Which one of us is handicapped?"

He had the last word. Whether he was referring to my lack of condition or whether he was suggesting I take off a few pounds, I never asked. But I've thought of Jack's story many times and used it on myself on many occasions—sometimes in situations where I make it through the fence, and sometimes when someone else does, and even sometimes when I'm the bull. It is amazing what you can learn from a twelve-year-old you are supposed to be teaching. We all learn these lessons whether we are married or single, whether the children are our own or someone else's.

On one occasion I worked on a fireside at which President Hugh B. Brown was to be the speaker. I was assigned to put some flowers in the chapel, but one of the committee members said "the Brethren" had vetoed flowers in the chapel. I thought that was one of the most amazing things I had heard—that "the Brethren" cared one way or the other. The committee member was adamant. Brother Alvin R. Dyer had visited her stake and had the flowers removed from the pulpit. On this one incident, the premise was set up. I listened, I thought about it, and then I went out and bought the flowers for the chapel. President Brown arrived and did not remove them.

Years later I was on a general board assignment to a stake in Idaho. The visiting authority was Elder Alvin R. Dyer. After the conference was over I sat with the others in the airport waiting for the flight home, wearing the corsage given to me by the host stake. I glanced around and noticed the visiting brethren had on boutonnieres, all of them—with one glaring exception. Elder Dyer did not.

"Brother Dyer, are you allergic to flowers?" I inquired.

"Yes," he answered, somewhat startled at the question. "How did you know?"

"Simple," I replied, "you don't have on a boutonniere. The Sunday School board member has one. The Young Men's board member has one. The Priesthood committee member has one, but you don't. No stake president is going to give them to all the visitors except the general authority. So I figured you must be allergic." I then told him about the fireside.

He smiled. "What did you do when she told you not to put any flowers in the chapel?"

"I put them in," I admitted.

"Well, the Church is not going to go too far wrong with rebels like you in it."

I am not suggesting that in every instance in life we ignore the sensibilities and advice of others and go and do what we like anyway. But we face these dichotomies daily. Single women must face them. Married women must face them, too. We cannot spend our lives doing what "someone" tells us without thinking about it for ourselves. We have to build our own premises, and they should be built on the rock.

My father was a person who respected the things that matter most, but he did not take himself too seriously and allowed all men the same privilege. I remember on one occasion the family had been out for a drive and on the way back we stopped behind another car at a stop sign. The driver of the car in front of us was a rather hesitant lady. She waited at the stop sign, looking to the left and looking to the right, waiting for a break in the flow of traffic so that she could go. She waited, and she waited. We waited behind her. She looked left, and she looked right. There were few cars in sight, but she still did not venture out. My father tapped his fingers on the steering wheel. Not only was she waiting for a break in the flow of traffic but she was apparently waiting until there was no traffic at all. My father's patience was finally stretched to its limit. He clutched the steering wheel and advised, "DO something, Madam, even if it's wrong!"

It is good to be cautious—but not too cautious. Decisions have to be made in this life whether we want to make them or not. We may often be like the lady at the stop sign—in a position where we have to decide for ourselves. Sometimes friends, sometimes husbands, are there to help; but when they are not, we can't be like that lady and just sit at the stop signs of life and do nothing.

One of the most valuable lessons of my life came inadvertently from a President of the Church. I was driving along State Street in Salt Lake City when a car pulled out in front of me, much to my annoyance and to my muttered comments. I gave the driver some well-deserved advice (which he was unaware of and which he did not take), and I thought all sorts of things about him until I pulled even with him at the stoplight. Suddenly I changed my tune completely. Now it was, "Oh, it's you, President McKay. That's quite all right, President McKay. Any time, President McKay." I was oozing with such servility that I made myself sick.

Now the problem with that kind of attitude toward life is that I am unconsciously accepting the fact that there are some people I am polite to and some people I am not polite to. Why did the driver have to be someone I knew before I allowed him a good thought or a good day? Making allowances for President McKay's driving was easy. Am I willing to make the same allowance for everyone?

Well, life teaches me lots of lessons and experiences refine me in ways I would not always choose if I wanted to be comfortable. Sometimes I make it through the fence, and sometimes I don't, but fortunately I have friends who help me. Some are married, and some are single. Some are deaf, and some are hearing. Some are black, and some are white. They help me, and I help them. We are all hanging in there trying to endure to the end and having a lot of fun along the way. For myself, I don't think being married would change that one iota.

Apricot Chutney

Marion Jane Cahoon

I grew up surrounded by the beauty of gardens. My father taught the practical and edible side of plants. Our vegetable garden was always planted on the fifteenth of May, and I grew to love the smell of earth as we prepared the soil. Father gave lessons on growing red and black raspberries, pruning trees, and roasting harvested English walnuts.

Mother taught different lessons. In her English country garden, I learned to love flowers. She reminded me of a music conductor. Different moods evolved in the garden beds as flowers changed from the delicate spring blossoms to summer and fall blooms. Mother knew when to have a clump of daisies spring up in time to take the place of a declining daffodil, and we enjoyed the constant color and beauty throughout the entire summer.

A garden is a wonderful metaphor for me because I believe in the law of the harvest. Selecting seeds, planting, watering, weeding, cultivating, and enjoying—harvesting and sharing—

Marion Jane Cahoon is a nutrition specialist and food publicity director. A home economist, nutritionist, lecturer, and culinary artist, she has made frequent guest appearances in the media. She earned her bachelor of science degree in family and consumer studies at the University of Utah. Her Church service has included membership on the Young Women General Board and a variety of other leadership and teaching positions.

all these elements of a beautiful garden are keys to a colorful, happy life.

I have learned how to plant seeds in my career, in my church work, and in my personal life. Not every seed grows as soon as I plant it, and some volunteer plants pop up to surprise me, but the Lord has always provided me with the constant flowering of good friends and opportunities to grow.

Some people favor gardens with clearly defined rows of petunias and marigolds and chrysanthemums. Often this orderly row attitude transfers to the way they view life—with marriage in the early twenties, children soon thereafter, and all other events falling neatly in line, row after row. My life hasn't proceeded like a formal garden, but my personal harvest is nonetheless rich and abundant.

As a single person, I've never been particularly depressed that my garden hasn't yielded a bridal bouquet yet. Instead of focusing on the flowers that aren't there, I've chosen to truly savor the flowers that have bloomed. The Lord has blessed me with a rich variety of challenges, people, and opportunities. I have a life like my mother's English country garden—full of drifts and banks and spots of variety, full of spiritual harvest, and some stubborn weeds that keep me on my knees.

Some blooms were cultivated opportunities; some were purely spontaneous. No matter how they came into my life, I have learned that my joy in the harvest increases when I focus on the beauty that is right at my feet instead of daydreaming about something else I'd like to see bloom in my life.

Whenever I cut fresh tiger lilies to arrange in a vase, I remember the owner of a gourmet cooking school who opened my eyes to food artistry. Attending a cooking school was a new adventure for me, and the large city I'd recently moved into offered many opportunities to be explored. Eagerly I telephoned the owner to ask all kinds of questions: What types of cooking classes were taught? How often? How many hours a session? She explained that class size was restricted to ten, allowing good hands-on experience for everyone. After each three-hour class, we would sit down to the feast we had created.

I nearly dropped the telephone when she gave the cost for the six-week series. I wanted to take all the courses but could barely afford one of them. While I listened to her explain the rest of what I needed to know to enroll, an idea popped into my head, and I asked her if she could use a dishwasher for the class. To my surprise, she said she possibly could use someone. Then she asked me to come in for an interview.

I arrived for the interview and was accepted for one to two nights each week (without pay) as the advanced French cooking class dishwasher. Never as a teenager would I have believed that being allowed to wash dishes would be such a privilege.

I piled the dishes in hot sudsy water and turned around periodically to absorb all the instruction the teacher gave until I needed to turn back to the assignment that got me there. Meanwhile, the room was filled with the savory smells of fresh fruit tarts and chocolate cheesecakes. I dried dishes while watching the teacher, perched atop a ladder, spin long golden strands of sugar across the end of a well-buttered broom handle.

In the next series, I was promoted to cook's assistant and found myself standing and stirring over the stove while learning about *crème anglaise* and reduction sauces. Someone else scoured away on the piles of pots and pans. I was offered a full-time job after a few more series (this time with pay) creating window displays and selling kitchen gadgetry imported from Europe.

A new experience now unfolded as I routinely met international chefs when they came to teach private classes. I stood at their sides and assisted—a glorified dishwasher again—but at the elbow of masters.

Two Spanish maids who didn't speak English became my dear friends. I collected authentic recipes while perched on a stool near the oak table, rapidly writing down the ingredients and instructions in Spanish. The maids showed me how to make fresh corn and flour tortillas, which we often ate for lunch. They cleaned out the refrigerator every week and masterfully made wonderful Spanish lunches from an assortment of odds and ends.

I noticed during these happy, learning months that the owner occasionally received a box of fresh tiger lilies. Some months the large blooms were pink, other months, deep amber. She placed the long stems in a tall vase on top of a credenza framed by a large french window. One day I asked her who repeatedly sent such elegant flowers. Smiling, she turned and said, "Me." I'm sure I looked a little surprised because she quickly explained she had a standing order with a neighborhood florist to send her a baker's dozen whenever the tiger lilies were particularly beautiful. "Who wants to receive them at your funeral when you can't smell them? I want to enjoy their fragrance while I'm alive," she added.

I'll not forget my year there. I'll never want to lose the memory of people or of the aromas that oozed out of every window and door. I remember, too, the copper pots hanging in the windows and reflecting sunlight, the peasant breads, the rich genoise with butter cream, the crepes, and the fresh pasta.

I learned something there of food as an art form. It was a blending of artistry and the practicality learned from my kitchen chemistry background at the university. When I left, the Spanish maids gave me a tortilla press. The whole adventure had started with dirty dishes, sudsy water, and a little elbow grease. When I see tiger lilies, I'm there again.

Fresh-growing basil reminds me of another friend who became my first mentor during my college years. I remember praying fervently one evening to have access always to great people and to be around those who inspired me to be better. Shortly afterwards, I met one of the most influential women in my life. We were thrown together during a college crusade to save the profession of home economics, but our professional connections grew into a delightful friendship.

Almost each time I went to visit I was greeted at the door with her request, "I need you to sample something for me." The day's creation could range from savory soup to strawberry sorbet. Although our adventures with food and recipes continued to bring us together, her kitchen cupboards also nourished my heart. Quotations, typed and taped up, reminded me to rejoice and renew.

From her kitchen we often retreated to another favorite room. Tucked away in a basement corner was her home office. The room was lined with three walls of shelves and stuffed with books. Whenever my mother groaned over my two large legal-size filing cabinets I would retort that my friend had seven. We operated like a lending library with our constant sharing of books, articles, and files.

I tested recipes for her while she was a food editor for the local newspaper. We sorted through the recipes readers had submitted to decide—on paper, before purchasing ingredients—what would or would not work. The final proof, however, was literally in the pudding: there was no way to know if something was good until it was made. There were a few recipes whose ingredient combinations sounded next to awful. When we came across these recipes, she was firm in saying, "Well, Marion, let's not slide over these quickly. There's something interesting and worthwhile to check out here." She was right. I remember one such recipe—apricot chutney. On my own I wouldn't have considered making it, but I found its flavor combination simply wonderful. It's now a favorite for both of us. I learned how easy it is to bypass something just because it is a little different.

I have since discovered that the lesson about apricot chutney is important in my personal life, too. Some of my experiences, at the outset, appeared much like apricot chutney—too unusual to consider sampling. But these surprises have added richness, variety, and unexpected delight to my life.

I learned another lesson from her. While testing for her cookbook, I discovered something about searching for quality. She said, "I have room in my life for only one excellent chocolate cake recipe." So I tackled the pile of "favorite" cake recipes (some ingredients varied by only a half cup of flour) to find the very best one. The neighbors loved lining up with plate and fork to munch through each sample and rate the taster's pick. We did end up with the best chocolate cake recipe, and we uncluttered our lives of the others.

One Christmas I gave my friend a bottle of whole nutmegs and a small nutmeg grater. During my previous adventures with food I had learned to use fresh herbs and spices. We were both amazed at the difference between the aroma of already ground spice and the fresh spice we grated directly into our recipes. She often said the fresh nutmeg had a hint of lemon to it.

We discovered the unsurpassable flavor of fresh herbs. I frequently gave her a sprig of basil from my herb garden to use with tomatoes. We decided that if we could have only one herb in our gardens it would have to be sweet basil. When adjusting our recipes, we substituted three tablespoons of fresh for each teaspoon dried, and we each purchased a mortar and pestle to crush the fragrant leaves. Her garden now grows several fresh basil plants each summer. I believe I taught her a little about using fresh herbs, basil in particular. Sharing with her taught me new ways to be a friend. It planted the seed of meaningful relationships in my own garden.

Whenever I see water lilies, I remember the day I learned about lily pads. It was during a family vacation with five other families in the mountains. One afternoon we hiked to a lake to fish and discovered a homemade raft moored on the side of the lake. The teenagers among us plopped down on logs and started talking. I wanted to get on that raft, but the older teenagers said they didn't want to get wet or cold. I was torn. My father said, "You can always get warm and dry again, Marion, but you won't always have pine logs, rafts, and lakes to explore." So my father, sister, and I set out to sea on the raft using our hands as paddles, splashing away. The water was clear and brisk. Ducks skimmed the surface and landed.

But I remember the day best for the lily pads in the middle of the lake. They were a mass of blooms and green, fanlike leaves. The lilies were so thick and dense it was possible to stand up on them and walk. Ankles slooshing in water, we ran on the waves on the tops of the lily pads. It was exhilarating to run the length of our plant island. We hopped gingerly at first but soon bounded with confidence. Later, on shore, I warmed up and dried off during the long walk back to the tent.

I've never forgotten that day. I've looked for lily pad islands ever since to run "on the wave" again, but never found them. I'm so glad I didn't stay warm and dry that day.

Eating cupcakes under apple trees reminds me of married friends and their families. That memory started when I craved a spice cake cupcake one August. To make one cupcake really meant a tray full, so I looked for friends who might enjoy them with me. Several days later we met for a "lunch and launch" party at the ice ponds of a community farm: husbands, wives, and children—all hungry for cupcakes.

Part of the day's activities included a flotilla of six toy sailboats I had collected to entertain nieces and nephews. The cloth sails could be adjusted: tight sails for strong breezes, or loose sails to gather a whisper of wind. The adjustable rudders could be set so the sailboat skimmed straight across the pond or traveled back to shore in a circle, boomerang style. Thirteen children, running from one side of the pond to the other, kept the water busy with the sailboat fleet. Moms and dads roamed the shore line ready to jump in after anyone who might accidentally fall into the pond.

The most fun was the boat-making contest. The children brought their own creation (with a little help from mom or dad) to the party. The children lined up, and as each one in turn raised a homemade boat over his or her head to show it to the group, we clapped our hands and shouted and cheered. Everyone was a winner. Once we put the boats to float, however, some immediately flipped over and became submarines. I learned that some of those fathers were chemists and real estate brokers—but not nautical engineers.

We ate our picnic under the broad limbs of an apple tree. The day was hot, but the apple tree gave wonderful shade. I needed to give away something of myself that day to my friends. Spice cake cupcakes always bring back memories of the day we launched the sailboats.

Orange and yellow aspen leaves remind me of my girlhood friends. During October three years ago, the seven of us were the only ones hiking up a mountain trail. The trail was dry and dusty as we started at the bottom of the valley floor, but as we knew it would, the trail wound higher into pines and aspens, over streams and waterfalls. Ten years had passed since we had all hiked up that trail together. But ten years earlier we had made a date with time. Now we were retrieving our time capsule.

As young girls we had hiked that canyon each summer from junior through senior high school. But after our first year of college, our paths separated into different directions. We wanted to do something fun that would bind us together, and so we decided to bury a time capsule in our favorite hiking canyon, capturing a moment of our lives and thoughts. We promised to make the trek again in ten years not only to retrieve our capsule but to bury a new one. Our plan was to continue gathering in the canyon each decade to unearth our time capsule for as long as we were able to hike the canyon.

We all wondered out loud if we could find the spot after ten years. Before we left, one friend's husband wagered a dinner that we couldn't do it. But the unusual geological rock formation we had carefully chosen earlier was easy to spot. We dug down deep into dark dirt. At three feet, the shovel clinked against the metal lid.

We opened the unbroken wax seal and laughed over the contents. There were silly predictions which (luckily) never came true. There were tender moments as we quietly read loving letters written by mothers and sisters. There was even a letter for all of us written by our friend who was the first of us to get married. She was married the week we buried the capsule. The letter told us how happy she was to have found the best man in the whole world and that we were all out of luck—he was already taken. She felt the same after ten years of marriage.

We really chuckled over the letter one friend had written to her future husband, who hadn't as yet materialized. It contained her goals and thoughts on what kind of woman she wanted to become for herself and for him during those ten years. After reading the letter to the mystery man, we slipped it into the new time capsule. The goals and dreams written of there were still good ones to continue seeking.

Surrounded by a forest of autumn leaves, we looked out over the same valley we had viewed many times before. Even as the leaves yearly changed into yellow and gold to make way for spring, our friendships continued to grow. These women have been good and gentle influences in my life.

Freesias, a favorite flower, evoke other tender memories. On top of my pie-safe cupboard rests a beautiful glass bowl. Freesias are handcut into the glass—flowers that never wilt. I've used that bowl to hold whole fruits, raspberry muffins, and fresh flowers and as an art piece polished to stand on the table by itself. The bowl was given to me by my adopted grandmother.

We became acquainted through a common friend. We came to an agreement early: I could call my new friend Grandma if I would visit her. I felt I won on both counts. I never felt close to my natural grandmothers because they either passed away when I was very young or lived so far away our paths crossed infrequently.

Her home is the grandmotherly type. The couch and chairs in the living room are all comfortable, the kind where you feel welcome to plop down and talk for long hours. But it is the kitchen I enjoy best. I learned to love parsnips there and ate many a hot roll dripping with her raspberry-cherry jam. It was a blue-ribbon recipe. Taking down her recipe instructions was always a little frustrating because she cooked to taste and from her heart and memory. I followed her around, peering over her shoulder, writing down what "a little of this and a little of that" meant in standard teaspoons, tablespoons, and cups.

While we prepared snacks to eat, Grandma talked to me of life. Once, when I was discussing some of my challenges and concerns, she said, "Every age has its compensation, Marion." I knew a little of her challenge to adapt her life after the passing of her husband. It was difficult to deal with loneliness, but she saw it as a time to do the writing she loved to do. Her second book was published this year.

Grandma also taught me lessons on a life of simplicity. I learned one of these while sitting down to a bowl of whole fresh strawberries with a touch of cream. "It would ruin those strawberries to do anything else to them," she would say. I thought of my own life, so jam-packed and tight with commitments—as tight as a bottle of pickled dilly beans—that it was nearly impossible to savor the individual events.

Grandma appreciated the common happenings of life I so often overlooked. I grew to understand that as I listened to her talk of fine china and dishes. She wrote down her thoughts for a community program honoring ancestors and heritage. She wrote, "Dishes carry tangibles like food and intangibles like memories and traditions." She explained to me how they carried cookies for a friend, a hot casserole for a funeral lunch, a pot of soup for a neighbor's needs, a pitcher of lemonade for the kids. Some dishes were for daily meals throughout the year; others were unique, such as a cherished grandmother's teapot that crossed a continent. To Grandma, whether those dishes were of the past or from the present, they stood for love, sharing, caring, family pride, and home.

One day she asked my advice on which plate would be best to arrange some banana nut bread in for a party. We went through every cupboard, starting in the kitchen and going through the china cupboard. We finally ended in the hall closet.

In our searching, one particular dish caught my eye. It was a large glass bowl, shallow but with a wide open rim. Its uses could be endless, and it was a beautiful art piece. She must have noticed how much I admired it. The next time I came to visit, my freesia bowl was wrapped up in a kitchen towel, peasant style. Grandma slipped it into my arms as I walked out to go home. "This is to remember me by," she said.

Bouquets of red and rose ranunculus remind me of a fleeting but meaningful friendship, half a world away in Egypt. Cairo is a city of contrasts. There is the obvious old and new. In one panoramic view of the city it is possible to see the great pyramids of Giza bordering the city on the west and twentieth-century buildings lining the banks of the Nile.

Cairo is also a dusty city. So little rain falls that the tree leaves are coated with dust. The whole city looks the same dull color. Such a dull background only makes fresh flowers stand out even more. Flower vendors are everywhere, and it is possible to purchase a dozen roses for a few dollars.

This love affair with flowers is an ancient one. I admired the great treasures of King Tutankamen but stood more in awe of what I suspect was the least noticed item from his tomb—a bunch of dried flowers. That funereal spray of fresh flowers was the last thing laid across his sarcophagus, perhaps by a loved one, before the door was sealed. After that, I began purchasing flowers, ranunculus, from the street vendors and wore the flowers in my hair.

One afternoon, several friends and I went to visit the mosque lady in old Cairo. She lived in a combination of three tents patched together just off the street on the porch of a mosque. Her tent was as city-dusted as the tree leaves. As we walked through the tent door opening, her face broke into a smile as she recognized one of her visitors. Almost before I was introduced to her, a young peasant boy darted through the tent door opening with soda pop and fresh bananas. My friend visited with her in broken Arabic and English while I munched on a banana. I reflected over the customs of this desert people while looking through the tent door onto the busy street.

Anciently, tent doors were left open among the desert people as a sign of hospitality to all travelers. Before retiring, the desert people searched the horizon to see if any traveler was on the desert. If visitors did arrive, they were invited in and offered food, drink, and clean clothes. A visitor's name was not asked nor the nature of his business until the visitor chose to discuss it.

I noticed, after a while, why the peasant boy was needed to run the errands. The mosque lady's swollen legs were like huge tree stumps. It would be very difficult for her to walk anywhere.

When we said our goodbyes, I wanted to give something to this kind woman who had so quietly and immediately accepted me as her friend. I took the flower from my hair and slipped it into hers.

The scent of pine boughs reminds me of the Christmas when I started a new family tradition under the pine trees at my parents' home.

My married brothers and their families always come to spend Christmas Eve at my parents' home. One year I warned them to come with galoshes and warm mittens. We would need to do some walking just before they left to go home. Curiosity ran high as the family gathered on the front porch. There my sister and I greeted them with tall red candles. We lit them and wound our way through the neighborhood, singing our favorite Christmas carols. As we left the last house, my sister and I led the way back toward home. We walked single file, singing under the starlit sky, crunching through the snow. Occasionally someone would shout, "Where are we going?" I didn't answer. After a while, they joined in and continued singing.

We wound our way past Mother's old-fashioned English garden. Two feet of snow now covered the flower beds. We continued winding down into Father's orchard past the English walnut tree and raspberry bushes. After turning a bend, we came upon the end of the singing journey. There, under a long graceful pine bough, protected from new-falling snow, was a manger scene gently lighted by our glowing candles. There we sang "Away in a Manger" with new meaning. One small toddler said, "Good night, baby Jesus" as we wound our way back up to cars to travel home.

Apple trees and spice cake cupcakes . . . Grandma's freesia bowl . . . a baker's dozen of tiger lilies . . . fresh basil . . . dusty Cairo and red ranunculus . . . pine boughs and a new tradition . . . lily pads and the splashing and leaping of an unforgettable day . . . yellow aspen leaves and ten years of memories . . . these are just a glimpse into my garden, into my life.

Life is seldom a formal garden. I have discovered that my own life is like an English country garden, where experiences and friendships are random and varied. My garden yields constant surprises. At times what I thought I planted grew to be something else. That happened one year in my father's garden with mismarked carrot seeds. We grew radishes instead. Now I've learned to delight in whatever grows and to look forward to each year's planting.

Instead of being worried over the Lord's timing, over the seasons and blooms and harvesting times in my garden, I have tried to simplify my approach by asking myself one question, one that Heavenly Father can give a confirmation to: "What is the next right thing to do?"

I have found that Heavenly Father has always shown me what flower is next, by confirming my choice of the next right thing to do, but he has not always shown me what will bloom next summer. Nevertheless, I have learned I can always count on him. I know that he doesn't neglect me; he is very much aware of my needs.

The Lord takes me in my context and teaches me. I have a married friend with a husband and three little boys. She and I have often delighted in the fact that the two of us have arrived at the same spiritual growth and insights, often within a few months of each other. We arrived at these truths through entirely different paths but emerged with the same convictions.

The Lord seems to know the condition of my garden, when a new flower is needed and where and how it should be planted. And I have learned to trust him as the Lord of the harvest.

Lessons from Algebra

Mary Kay Stout

There was nothing I wanted more to avoid than taking algebra in junior high school. A victim of the new math, I dreaded algebra. But to my delight, on the first day of class I discovered that the answers to all the problems were in the back of the book. I was surprised, relieved, and puzzled. I thought, "Why didn't someone do this sooner? But what will we be doing all year since we already have the answers?"

What I learned in algebra was the process of moving from complex problems to solutions, that is, to the answers in the back of the book. But though the problems were clearly stated and the answers too, success in algebra required skills in the process of learning and using mathematical principles. I soon learned that skipping steps and taking shortcuts created difficulties. Having the answers was convenient, and it helped me know whether I was on track, but I soon discovered that there were frequently several ways to solve a problem, depending on the mathematical approach. The process and the steps in problem-solving were critical to understanding the right answer. I learned to recognize that the answers in my text were meaningless if I

Mary Kay Stout is a senior project manager with a management consulting firm. She received her education at Brigham Young University and at the University of California at Los Angeles. She has served in ward and stake leadership and teaching positions in Relief Society and Young Women. She has also served as a seminary teacher in her area.

did not go through the challenge of learning to move from problem to solution.

Assuming that because the answers are given, the process will be easy, is a misconception not restricted to junior high algebra. I still find myself skipping steps, looking for shortcuts, or wanting to jump directly to an answer. Yet I am becoming better able to see the difficulties in achieving a fit between a problem ("I don't get along with my boss") and the gospel's answers ("Love your neighbor"). How to link the two is not always apparent. It is easy to resent the transition between a problem and the gospel's answer because it may require the challenge of applying the principles to reach a solution.

I survived junior high algebra. I learned that as appealing as those easily obtainable answers had been at first, they were not going to rescue me from learning and applying principles. I also found that some errors consistently crept into my work and that certain types of problems created predictable barriers to my reaching solutions.

As with my encounter with algebra, my experiences with learning to live the gospel have revealed a catalog of recurring barriers that make the process of moving from problems to solutions particularly difficult. Some of these barriers are rooted in false expectations, poor logic, and bad habits. Many of these barriers I observe in other single Church members as well as in myself; however, they are not unique to single Latter-day Saints. They present difficulties to married Latter-day Saints as well, and to single and married nonmembers. We do well to recognize that generally the scriptures emphasize our true commonality of experience and interest by addressing us as individuals rather than as members of particular groups or categories. Likewise, we need to acknowledge that male and female, Church member and nonmember, married and single, we confront common barriers to progress. Regardless of its source, each barrier presents unique obstacles in moving from problems to solutions. I have found it helpful to try to recognize these barriers and examine how they may thwart the problem-solving process.

Entitlement

The expectation of a cause-and-effect relationship frequently produces an assumption that we have earned, deserve, or are entitled to a specific reward such as marriage, financial security, happiness, career success, or friendships because of personal worthiness or sacrifice. Although cause-and-effect applies in many circumstances (obtaining educational degrees, or strengthening muscles), it does not necessarily apply either in building relationships with others or in receiving blessings from our Heavenly Father.

A belief in entitlement may result in disillusionment if we feel we have not received the fulfillment and growth we have earned almost as if by contract. It is easy for us to convince ourselves that we have earned rewards according to our own timetables. "I've been righteous, faithful, and chaste! Where are my blessings?"

The consequences of an entitlement mind-set are varied. We may feel shortchanged by our Heavenly Father and question whether he is honoring his end of an agreement when blessings do not come on our schedule or on our terms. In addition, failing to recognize the source and extent of our blessings, we may apply a cause-and-effect formula to determine expected rewards. We may also fail to recognize the Lord's blessings to us because they may not be the ones we have previously determined we want or deserve. We may fail to distinguish between what we may desire (marriage and children now) with what we have been promised (the blessings of Abraham and eternal life). Lastly, belief in entitlement with its I've-got-it-coming-to-me attitude attacks essential elements of the gospel, including humility, gratitude, and dependence on the Lord.

The behavioral consequences of the entitlement expectation have been played out in wards throughout the Church. When our Heavenly Father fails to respond like a short-order cook filling requests, many individuals have become disgruntled and have felt that their Heavenly Father does not know their needs or love them. They feel that because he has failed to deliver on his end of some imaginary deal, they no longer feel obligated to honor their end. ("I've been faithful, and what good has it done me?") Feeling shortchanged, some have abandoned personal convictions, covenants, and activity in the Church. Some have assumed they are unworthy or less loved than others. It is not the expectation that the Lord will bless us that results in dysfunctional assumptions; rather, it is the expectation of our right to determine the timetable, extent, and nature of the blessings.

Swimming Against the Current

Closely related to the concept of entitlement is the basic incongruity between what we profess ("Life is a continual series of challenges to face and overcome") and what we actually believe and its influence on our decision making ("If I could only find a better job . . . buy a home . . . lose fifteen pounds . . . get him to like me, I would be happy"). We are taught that life is an upstream swim. We are swimming against the current. Our progress may not always be steady, or we may momentarily drift downstream, or we may need to stop and rest. The current against which we swim may flow from within ourselves or from external challenges or adversities. For most of us, this concept is difficult to embrace. I remember thinking, "If only I were thinner, I would be happier and more enthusiastic, outgoing, and cheerful." During several months of diligent dieting and exercise, I watched unwanted pounds drop and expected them to be replaced by sterling character traits. I found, however, that although I was indeed thinner, I wasn't necessarily any happier or more enthusiastic, outgoing, or cheerful. Achieving one goal didn't mean automatically achieving others.

I could see that reaching that one goal did not magically eliminate all other challenges in my life. I wanted to believe that losing weight would result in a new and improved me. Somehow the combination of diet and exercise would eliminate the bad habits and weaknesses of many years' standing. Finally I was forced to abandon the conviction that there might be a sure, magical combination that would crack the safe containing the prize of guaranteed happiness. I have come to realize that we generally try many combinations in attempting to open the stubborn lock, convinced we will come across the right one if only we keep trying.

Although identifying the sought-after rewards contained in the safe is rather straightforward (feeling loved, rearing children in the faith, achieving professional respect), reaching the contents of the safe is difficult. We listen to friends' accounts of the perfect job, the diet to end all diets, the ultimate exercise program, and Mr. Right. The search is for the correct combination to the safe that will yield self-fulfillment, attractiveness, good health, and a happy life. Even when the perfect job turns sour, crash diets fail, or a relationship evaporates, we frequently persist in our safecracking methods. We seem unwilling to abandon the search for magical access to the blessings we seek.

As the children of Israel hungered for the flesh pots of Egypt (see Exodus 16:3), we stand convinced that satisfying one need in our lives will make us truly happy. The Lord's gift of quail did not improve the Israelites' dispositions or soften their hardened hearts; neither will a sure, one-shot solution be satisfying or growth-sustaining for us.

Safecracking is a two-edged sword. It does encourage us to focus our energies on a specific problem or concern. When we are seeking the safe's combination, we remain in a problem-solving mode, open to new methods of obtaining rewards, rather than shotgunning in a random and haphazard manner; however, safecracking presents some problems. It creates in us the false expectation that there are simple and magical answers that produce the rewards we value. We may concentrate on one desired reward to the exclusion of other worthwhile rewards and goals. When we fail to expect an upstream swim, we may not anticipate or appropriately deal with the strong and steady current. We may deceive ourselves by thinking that knowing the combination and receiving the reward will make us happy forever and eliminate or enable us to deal with challenges. While the sought-after rewards may be worthwhile, repeatedly attempting combinations may wear on our patience and make us less willing to continue to pursue growth.

The behavior of individuals in search of the right combinations to safes may involve varied patterns, including lack of staying power and a tendency to impulsive actions. Consequences might range from spotty employment records and frequent requests for releases from Church callings to fad health programs and get-rich-quick financial schemes, none of which helps us understand that the process of growth on this earth is "line upon line, precept upon precept." (D&C 98:12.)

Horribilizing

I always knew that I wanted to go to graduate school. Yet as the time grew closer to apply for admission, I started to say to myself, "I have to take the Graduate Management Admissions Test before I can apply. I don't think I will do well, and I probably won't be accepted at a good graduate school. I guess I will be in this job forever." Before I even so much as sent for an application, I had convinced myself that I would be rejected.

Because we frequently place enormous importance on single events or outcomes, we may fall victim to horribilizing: forecasting the worst possible outcome and making decisions as if it had already taken place. While the scenario is actually hypothetical, we act as if what we fear were already a fait accompli. Negative forecasting sets in motion a sequence of decisions and actions that cripples our abilities.

Consider my graduate school example: I had forecast low test scores followed by rejected applications. I was narrowing my options by convincing myself that I would fail. The basis for my decision was not sound evidence but merely an expectation of failure. The perception of horrible outcomes blocked my ability to make decisions and take action in pursuit of a goal, a graduate degree.

Horribilizing is often dysfunctional, but it can serve functional purposes. There are situations in which creating a negative forecast is helpful. Recognizing negative scenarios may prevent such unwise conduct as reckless driving, violations of the Word of Wisdom, and income tax evasion. By convincing us that effort is futile, however, horribilizing can severely limit our ability to grow and learn. Many of us remain in dead-end jobs, pass over prudent financial investments, or miss travel opportunities because of our propensity to presume failure.

Failure to make decisions and take risks sets us up for discouragement and a sense of victimization. We need to remember that the Lord has admonished us, "For with God nothing shall be impossible." (Luke 1:37; see also Genesis 18:14.)

Overwhelming Tasks

Recently my young nephew and I had a tug-of-war over which of us was going to pick up and put away his toys. I requested, reasoned, bargained, and offered to help, all to no avail. He was not going to pick up his toys regardless of my schemes to get him to do so. Finally his mother, amused by my efforts, said, "Picking up the toys is an overwhelming task to him. He doesn't think he can do it."

I decided to turn the situation into a game. "Charlie, see how fast you can put all the green blocks into the box. I'll pick up the yellow blocks, and we'll race each other." Charlie darted around the room picking up green blocks while I scrambled to find yellow ones. We repeated our contest until all the toys had been put away.

What I had viewed in Charlie as stubbornness and laziness was actually difficulty in dividing work into discrete tasks that could be accomplished one at a time. Picking up a room full of scattered toys really was an overwhelming task for him. Rather than begin and fail, he resisted my proddings that he start until he was convinced he would succeed. Once he was given specific, limited tasks, he jumped in with excitement.

The example of Charlie and the blocks is one that has helped me understand how many of us approach overwhelming tasks. In Charlie's case, once I understood his reluctance, I could see how to divide the work into manageable steps. Yet I often fail to do that in my own life. We struggle to understand how to divide what we perceive as an overwhelming task (getting out of debt, owning a home, or researching genealogy) into small, incremental steps. Yet, the inability to do so means we may continue to live with the same problems, conflicts, and bad habits year after year.

Overwhelmed individuals may cope with a problem by avoiding, rationalizing, or procrastinating. It is easy to become cynical when hearing talks in church on setting goals, managing our time, and overcoming self-defeating behaviors after we have listed (or failed to list) the same January 1 goals for several years running. We frequently convince ourselves that the task will remain unapproachable and insurmountable. Many individuals who regard themselves as professionally and socially competent will admit that there are touchy issues in their personal lives that have not benefited from their formidable skills. Many of us have not developed manageable working plans for our personal equivalents to cleaning out the garage.

The Art of Plate Spinning

As a child I used to watch the *Ed Sullivan Show* and was fascinated by men spinning plates on long poles. The rules were simple: spin as many plates as possible; give attention to the plate that is most off balance; you are out at the first crash. The skill of a plate spinner was measured by how many plates he could keep in motion without a mishap.

Each of us is spinning plates, but not with long poles and fine china. We are using calendars, meetings, agendas, reports, projects, and activities of every kind. I have come to recognize the danger of comparing myself with others. Significant misjudgments are likely if I compare quantity, speed, timing, and style. In reality, all plates are not equally difficult for each of us to keep in motion. Some plates will require full attention. We will likely become more adept as we acquire greater skill. Comparisons with those of greater experience can be discouraging.

It didn't happen often, but even Ed Sullivan's plate spinners occasionally were not quick enough to keep a plate from crashing to the floor. Good plate spinners also become adept at judging the number of plates they can spin successfully. They do not attempt to keep more plates in motion than they are able to, at least not on network television.

At times I find myself spinning more plates than I am able to manage successfully. Having experienced a few crashes and near-crashes, I know I am not always a good judge of how many I should try to set in motion. I have friends and family members who are more adept at this juggling act than I. One friend is particularly adroit, publishing in professional journals, teaching at a major university, consulting nationwide, and serving in Church leadership positions. It would be easy to become envious or discouraged because of my friend's accomplishments. Instead, I have tried to respect my friend's achievements rather than setting them up as benchmarks for measuring my own progress. In contrast, another friend is the first to volunteer for every new project or work assignment. Gradually she has developed the reputation for overcommitting herself: she backs out of responsibilities or requires others to rescue her. Managing the balancing act that each of us faces requires knowledge of our own abilities as well as patience and experience.

The Cafeteria Approach

One of the more popular and recent changes in large organizations is the shift away from uniform employee benefits to a so-called cafeteria approach. A company offers a wide assortment of benefits from which employees may select those most appealing or suitable to their circumstances. For example, one person may elect to forgo dental insurance in favor of increased pension contributions. Another may give higher priority to accruing sick days over vacation leave.

While a cafeteria-style program of employee benefits with its opportunity for customizing is attractive to employees, this same approach proves damaging when applied to the gospel. To our occasional dismay, the gospel is a "package deal." I cannot decide to select prayer, fasting, temple work, and the Word of Wisdom, and yet pass over tithing, consecration, chastity, or genealogy. Likewise, adopting the cafeteria approach is inappropriate to serving in the Church. We are not given the opportunity to sign up for specific Church callings to our liking while passing over those we view as less suitable or interesting.

I have friends who consider themselves good Church members and yet have identified issues on which they disagree with the principles of the gospel or the formally stated position of the Church. One argues against the Church's position on premarital sex and has broken her temple covenants. Another struggles with alcoholism and views the disease's repercussions as strictly physiological. A third stopped attending temple sessions because of her perception of the portrayal of women in the endowment ceremony. They state that their relationships with the Church would be vastly improved were the Church to broaden its perspective on their specific issues. They testify to the truthfulness of prayer, fasting, service, or other gospel principles; however, their unwillingness to see the gospel as a package deal and their persistence in selecting only certain principles and programs has caused each one to succumb to individual weaknesses and appetites.

All the Right Messages to All the Wrong People

Members of a ward Relief Society presidency in which I once served used to joke that we were going to publish a list of novel ways to say no to a request for Church work ("My oven's too small." "I'm sure I couldn't even find the cannery." "Couldn't we call a caterer?"). At other times we expressed concern that some ward members would willingly accept many responsibilities without informing anyone of the weight of their other tasks.

I have observed these contrasting responses frequently and have determined that the right messages are being received by the wrong people. Church members already engaged in good works may be the ones who take to heart counsel about the continued need for more good works. Messages that "it is not requisite that a man should run faster than he has strength" (Mosiah 4:27) are frequently heard most clearly by those not noted for Church service. Likewise, counsel to increase self-reliance is taken by those who have already adopted the practice, while counsel to increase faith is accepted by those who may need a nudge toward greater works.

Counsel from the scriptures and Church leaders is needed by the Latter-day Saints. Yet we often engage in selective neglect and selective magnification. We use scriptures and counsel from Church leaders as ammunition to defend our position and attack those who disagree with us. We feel justified in pursuing our self-selected virtues if we can find doctrinal support.

Virtues can be carried to extremes: the over-zealous concern for financial preparedness that promotes greed, the exercise program that feeds vanity, the genealogical typing undertaken during work hours, or the self-improvement course that turns an individual inward.

When right messages overly influence the wrong people, lives become distorted. We excel in some areas at enormous expense to others. Without doctrinal authority, we may decide some aspects of the gospel are optional, yet give other principles great attention. At times this approach is appropriate and produces growth. At other times it provides an excuse for missing church meetings, saying no to church callings, and turning down opportunities for service.

We may view some aspects of the gospel as more elective than others. We may decide that Sabbath rest is required but attendance at sacrament meeting is optional. Ultimately these rationalizations damage ourselves and others. Often we find in ourselves discrepancies between our conduct or attitude and a principle of the gospel. In trying to narrow the distance, we often enlarge it by placing inappropriate emphasis on another gospel principle.

When we disregard the levels and gauges of the gospel—the scriptures and counsel of Church leaders—and decide instead to eyeball it according to what feels right, even a strong foundation will not stand. The gospel is the steady guide that reveals our own misjudgments. When discrepancies exist between readings from a true level and our own attempts at eyeballing, we learn from experience which one to trust. Regardless of our instincts and our skill at eyeballing, the accuracy of the level remains constant. By trueing our lives with the gospel, we avoid faulty personal judgments based on our miscalculation and bias.

I Believe in the Gospel—It's Just the Church I'm Having Trouble With

My sister Helen Claire has decided that I am a theoretical cook. She says, "You have every cookbook imaginable and all the right equipment, but not much arrives on the table."

Somehow I have more enthusiasm for the culinary arts when I am in a bookstore than when I am in a kitchen. The concept of cooking, with images of ethnic and regional specialties full of exotic ingredients, is significantly more appealing than the reality of scouring pots and pans. Clearly an understanding of theory does not necessarily assure action.

As my sister's term "theoretical cook" indicates, the contrast between ideology and practice can result in simultaneous advocacy and inaction. In some areas, contributions may be made by developing theories and presenting ideas. In others, theorizing is unhelpful. The I-believe-in-the-gospel-it's-just-the-Church-I'm-having-trouble-with philosophy grows out of an inappropriate separation of theory and practice.

We invent variations on this theme: the gospel is "pure," but the Church is "political"; we desire Christlike love, yet dread home teaching; we sustain the Lord's anointed, yet suppose "Salt Lake doesn't know what it's doing." The problem does not lie in accepting the "new wine"; however, trading in the "old bottles" for new ones frequently proves difficult. (See Luke 5:37–39.)

For many, it is frequently more stimulating and enjoyable to theorize about problems than to rectify them. Others may be more inclined to take action and less prone to analyze. Of course, these activities are not mutually exclusive. Yet, many of us tend to do more of one than of the other. Frequently both sides have difficulty recognizing the contributions of the other. At best, each side may view itself as unappreciated and misunderstood; at worst, each regards the other as a threatening force. Building unity and strength despite diverse perspectives is difficult, especially when motives are challenged. When our own motive ceases to be building the kingdom, we must question the purpose of our theorizing and probing.

Most of us "kick against the pricks" more subtly than did Saul of Tarsus. (Acts 9:5; see also D&C 121:38.) Ark steadying frequently takes the guise of helpful actions. (See 2 Samuel 6:6.) We even invent rationales that allow us to steady the Church: "This isn't the Wasatch Front"; "The bishop has never been divorced"; "The manual doesn't meet the needs of the sisters." In such cases, the subject under subtle attack is not the gospel of Jesus Christ but the formal Church organization and its programs.

We may not even be conscious of the conversations, periodicals and other publications, and organizations we support that engage in Church-bashing. Although we openly raise our hands to sustain ward, stake, and Church leaders, our theorizing and challenging may undermine their authority and effectiveness and ultimately impair the growth of the Church. When this probing is conducted in public, we jeopardize ourselves to an even greater degree.

I do not mean to say that as Church members we should not rigorously examine our doctrines and programs. Nor do I imply that the formal Church itself will not continue to change to meet new concerns as well as address old ones. Yet there is a point at which neither we as individuals nor the Church as a whole will benefit from unbridled criticism. Perhaps because we view the Church as strong and enduring we believe it can withstand this gentle clubbing. Experience has taught me that Church-bashing jeopardizes not the Church but the individuals who engage in it. We often seem unwilling to anticipate the consequences of our actions on both members and nonmembers, who are neither as sturdy nor as enduring as the Church corpus itself.

I believe strongly that as Latter-day Saints we must find appropriate ways both to speak and to listen to those who encourage change within the Church. This exchange, however, contrasts sharply with situations in the Church when those who are thoughtless criticize those in authority or demand that they defend their actions.

When facing opposition to rebuilding the temple in Jerusalem, Nehemiah and his followers continued their steady work on the walls. Yet "every one with one of his hands wrought in the work, and with the other hand held a weapon." (Nehemiah 4:17.) Clearly the work would have proceeded more quickly had their challenge been limited to building rather than including defending as well. The prophet could not be distracted from the work. He sent a message to his critics, "I am doing a great work, so that I cannot come down." (Nehemiah 6:3.)

Today Church leaders continue the work of building temples and directing Church programs. They meet opposition as well. Their time is not well spent interrupting the Lord's work to justify their actions to faultfinders. I have gradually come to recognize the responsibility each of us has to use caution in our theorizing and efforts to bring about change so that our activities do not become murmuring and ark steadying.

If-Then Statements Revisited

"I don't have a testimony of home teaching."

"I don't see why I should have to write a journal."

"I don't believe in the practicability of a year's supply."

Generally such statements follow the acknowledging that in fact, the individuals do not home teach, keep a journal, or store a year's supply of food. It does seem logical: Why engage in activities when you question their value? Isn't it better to resolve the conflict within yourself and not be a hypocrite?

Most of us say that faith must precede any miracle, but we ignore the action that embodies that faith. I used to believe that faith was something we felt, and the miracle that would follow was something we saw. My experience has been that we see faith (in terms of actions taken) and feel the miracle (increased testimony, understanding). *If* we demonstrate faith, *then* we feel the Lord's hand in our lives.

The scriptures are explicit in outlining this if-then process. Throughout the standard works, what we must do (a commandment) is followed by a promise (a consequence). "If ye keep my commandments, ye shall abide in my love; even as I have kept my Father's commandments, and abide in his love." (John 15:10.)

If we obey the Word of Wisdom, then we "shall run and not be weary, and shall walk and not faint." (D&C 89:20.) If we are steadfast ("continue in my word"), then we will "know the truth." (John 8:31–32.) Yet frequently we expect to know the truth or receive the promised reward before we obey the law. Doing the right thing for the wrong reasons may frequently be the first step toward doing the right thing for the right reason.

When Answers Lead to New Problems

Back on that first day of algebra in junior high, I felt very smug. After all, I had all the answers in the back of my book. Having the right answers did prove to be a yardstick for measuring my understanding and abilities. I was able to rethink problems and attempt new solutions when my answers did not match the book's. All of this was valuable in teaching me to solve problems. But having right answers, whether to algebra problems or the larger issues of life, may, in itself, present challenges. In algebra, I found that I was not careful and was prone to take shortcuts because I could always go back and fix my work if my answer was wrong. And I found that I was not confident in my ability to solve problems when the answers were not available. Likewise, having the answers to gospel questions may make us more likely to expect that the search and struggle are over. We may take the answers to gospel questions for granted. Or we may become quick to match any answer to any problem regardless of the fit. We may diminish the importance of the process of overcoming difficulties because we already have answers. We may not recognize that frequently there are multiple right answers, some with better outcomes than others. And having answers may affect our relationship with those who have different answers or wrong answers.

Algebra, even with the answers in the back of the book, never proved to be the snap course I thought it would be. Yet I grew to appreciate its order and logic. I began to see how it was built upon a solid foundation of principles that were interrelated and could be combined to solve complex problems.

Having answers is a source of great strength, comfort, and direction. Consulting the answer book is even more important in building a successful life than in mastering algebra. The answers provided by the plan of salvation and the gospel give us the assurance that there is purpose to our questions and meaning in the problem-solving process. I believe that the blessings of the gospel of Jesus Christ are not limited only to some segments of the earth's population. The concept that we should expect to defer happiness until the next life and just remain faithful is riddled with false assumptions about a loving Heavenly Father and how he chooses to bless his children. Understanding the gospel of Jesus Christ and living its principles will make any person happier in this life and in the life to come.

Coming to Terms

Ida Smith

Several months ago a woman friend who is divorced and a convert to the Church was asked by a nonmember friend: "What does your church do for its single members?" My friend was not sure how to answer the question and posed it to me. I told her I did not have The Answer to that question and could only share with her how I would have answered it for me. My reply would have been, "Nothing. My church does not do anything for me as a single person."

But I believe the wrong question was asked. The question should have been: "What does the gospel of Jesus Christ as taught by your church do for you as a single person?" To that I would have replied, "Everything! It gives me a raison d'être, a yardstick by which to measure every decision, a vehicle to help me cope, a blueprint to follow to plan and build my life."

President Kimball said in his message to women in September 1979: "There is no greater and more glorious set of promises given to women than those which come through the gospel and the Church of Jesus Christ. Where else can you learn who

Ida Smith is the coordinator of Student/Alumni Programs at Brigham Young University and was founding director of the Women's Research Institute there. She earned her bachelor of arts degree in political science at the University of Utah and is a doctoral candidate at the Union Graduate School. Her Church callings have included ward and stake leadership and teaching positions in Relief Society, Special Interest, and MIA. She has also served as a Gospel Doctrine teacher.

you really are? Where else can you be given the necessary explanations and assurances about the nature of life? From what other source can you learn about your own uniqueness and identity? From whom else could you learn of our Father in Heaven's glorious plan of happiness?" ("The Role of Righteous Women," *Ensign*, Nov. 1979, p. 103.)

The Church is composed of over six million people who are striving—and succeeding at tremendously varied rates—to prepare to meet again their God and Creator. The scriptures warn us not to rely on the "arm of flesh" (D&C 1:19) because to do so we would doom ourselves at some point to become disappointed, disillusioned, or disaffected. In my seven years in leadership positions in the Church's Special Interest program in the San Francisco Bay Region and during five years as director of the Women's Research Institute at Brigham Young University, I have had ample opportunity to see and talk with many women who have indeed become disappointed, discouraged, disillusioned, and disaffected because of their experiences with the institutional church—either because they were women or because they were single.

Being of a basically stubborn nature, I determined years ago I would not allow anybody to drive me away from *my* church. Single, married, widowed, or divorced, I felt I had as much right and claim to it as any other person—and no one was going to take it away from me or drive me out. In the process of making that decision I learned to separate the "church," that is, individuals and institutional practices, from the "gospel," that is, eternal principles and doctrine.

A number of years ago when I was dealing with priesthood-bearing authorities in a situation that was particularly painful for me, I made a deliberate decision for myself: I covenanted with the Lord that I would do everything in my power to help bring about positive changes for women from *within* the Church. I vowed I would not leave it nor take pot shots at it from without as a number of individuals had chosen to do.

I have not allowed myself to view my single status from any other than a gospel perspective. Had I done so I would very possibly have given in in some life situations and would certainly have experienced more than my share of depression. I find it impossible not to deal with my femaleness as well as my singleness, and for me, how I deal with both must be within a gospel framework.

Because women are not in the official church reporting line, it is possible—and indeed it happens—for women living alone to learn of ward or church events after the fact. The assumption that priesthood bearers will share with their families information and announcements that are given only in priesthood meetings is not automatically realized, and the single woman is often left with no pipeline for information that has been given only to priesthood bearers.

Being thus invisible has, at times, been very painful for me, and I know it has been for other single women as well as for married women with nonmember or less active husbands. It is especially painful when we desire to be counted and recognized by our fellowmen as well as by our Father in Heaven.

My reactions over the years to many of the attitudes and practices of Church members have ranged from irritation and annoyance to anger and dismay. I frequently have found myself thanking my Father in Heaven for my single blessedness as I have tried to absorb the pain expressed by women suffering at the hands of priesthood-bearing husbands or Church authorities exercising unrighteous dominion. Whatever negatives I might have experienced personally have at least not been within the circle of my own home.

I believe that I am a daughter of Eve and that that condition is a positive one, not a negative one. I believe that Adam and Eve were glorified, equal beings in the Garden of Eden, that they both walked and talked with God, were equally yoked, equally loved by the Lord. I believe with Nephi that "all things which have been given of God from the beginning of the world, unto man, are the typifying, of him [Christ]" (2 Nephi 11:4), and therefore I believe that both Adam and Eve are types of Christ. Eve loved her unborn posterity enough to give her life's efforts that man might be; the Savior gave his life that man might be redeemed.

The Lord described to Adam and Eve the reality of what the Fall would mean to their posterity: the sufferings, the joys, the contentions, the triumphs, the evildoings, the opportunities for doing good. Part of that reality was that women would be subject to men. And when Christ came in the meridian of time, he would atone for the sins of Eve as well as for the sins of Adam.

I believe, as a woman, that I am important to and loved by my Father and Mother in Heaven—all alone, by myself, without husband and without children. Our goal as a people should be to emulate the equal partnership of Adam and Eve before the Fall, not to perpetuate the spiritually blind, unequal relationship that resulted from the Fall. If we are to strive to perfect ourselves so that we might receive a celestial glory hereafter, we should at least attempt to pattern our lives on a celestial model during our earthly probation. We should be men and women as the Savior taught: equal, not one ancillary to the other.

My personal definition of *feminist* is any man or woman who is concerned about the status of women. According to this definition, I believe the Savior is the greatest feminist of all time. Everything the Savior taught and did speaks to me of his belief in the equality of the sexes. Our record of him in the New Testament came through a highly patriarchal Jewish culture that was very negative, to my way of thinking, toward women. It is a powerful testimony to me of the status of women in the eyes of the Lord that his love and esteem for us survived the translations. A few examples are worth noting here.

The person to whom Christ first disclosed his true identity was a woman who was both Samaritan and harlot. (See John 4.) He spoke to her in a public place and then sent her forth as a witness to his identity and ministry. In this simple action Christ broke three major Jewish taboos: He spoke to a woman in public (in a culture where men were advised not to have overabundant speech with women, and *never* in public), interacted with a Samaritan, and used a woman as a witness.

Women were his friends, companions, and close associates, and some provided for him out of their own resources. Martha, for example, a homeowner in her own right, offered him refuge and sustenance. He neither kept women from his company nor kept them from attending his person. I believe he greeted the Saints—men, women, and children, as Paul later described—with a holy kiss, much, I would guess, as President Spencer W. Kimball greeted everyone.

Christ gave his body, not just on the cross, but in his life, as he submitted to the ministrations of his disciples and followers. On one occasion he allowed a woman to anoint his head and feet. On another he submitted to the ministrations of a woman, a known sinner, who bathed his feet with her tears and wiped them with her hair. (See Luke 7:37–39.) We also have record of John resting his head on the Savior's breast. (See John 13:23.)

Women were among his followers all during his ministry. They stood with him at the cross. He punctuated the most important single event in recorded history, his resurrection, by appearing first to women. (See Mark 16:9; John 20:13–16.) As one author phrased it:

"In typical male Palestinian style, the Eleven refused to believe the woman [regarding the resurrection] since, according to Judaic law, women were not allowed to bear legal witness. As one learned in the Law, Jesus obviously was aware of this stricture. His first appearing to and commissioning women to bear witness to the most important event of his career could not have been anything but deliberate: it was clearly a dramatic linking of a very clear rejection of the second-class status of women with the center of His Gospel, His resurrection. The effort of Jesus to centrally connect these two points is so obvious that it is an overwhelming tribute to man's intellectual myopia not to have discerned it effectively in two thousand years." (Leonard Swidler, "Jesus Was a Feminist," *Catholic World*, Jan. 1971, p. 177.)

The Savior met and accepted men and women where they were. For example, Christ asked Peter, "Lovest thou me?" using the word for the highest form of love in Greek, *agape*, or godlike love. Elder Bruce R. McConkie noted that twice Peter answered with *philia*, love of friends. (See John 21:15–17.) The third time the Savior asked the question, He met Peter where he was and used *philia* as well. This approach deals with things "as they are" (D&C 93:24) rather than as shoulds or oughts, which are really only devices we use to avoid the reality of what is.

I find that when men and women follow the Savior's example, they do not merely tolerate each other but seek to establish equitable relationships and to practice nurturing and submitting between them according to the strengths and infirmities of each other. In such relationships, regardless of age, status, or accomplishment, I do not feel put down, trivialized, or unseen by men, priesthood-bearing or otherwise.

When men in the institutional church comprehend, internalize, and exemplify the Savior's relationship with women, I observe the following things occur in the interrelations of men and women: Both exercise their imagination on behalf of the other person to try to discover the other's perspective; both do more listening than telling; both take upon themselves the burdens of their sisters or brothers that they "may be filled with mercy, . . . that [they] may know . . . how to succor . . . according to their infirmities" (Alma 7:12) rather than merely according to their own convenience or personal strengths.

The story is told of an explorer who came across a group of natives deep inside a rain forest. Because of the density of the foliage, the natives' perception had never exceeded twelve to fourteen feet. The explorer took them to the edge of the forest, and for the first time they were able to see a great distance. Two miles away were some water buffaloes. The explorer asked, "What are those?"

The natives replied, "They are ants."

"No," said the explorer, "they are water buffaloes." The explorer then took the natives the two miles' distance, and the natives discovered that the figures were indeed water buffaloes and not ants.

We are all raised in rain forests of one sort or another and therefore all run the risk of some time or another mistaking water buffaloes for ants and vice versa. As a result, we tend to believe not only that the world *is* the way we perceive it but also that that is the way the world *ought* to be.

As a single woman I have experienced some of the following rain forests:

A woman is nothing without a man, and a woman will be an old maid if she is not married by the time she is twenty-one.

Only unattractive women, or women who are not capable of getting a husband, go on a mission.

If a woman does not marry, either something is wrong with her, or she has done something bad, or God does not love her.

Divorced women are a threat to intact marriages, and single men are a threat to society.

If families are the norm, single people must be the abnorm and are therefore second class.

My father once said to me that as a single person I would never experience the highs that a person can reach only if married. By the same token, he said, I would never experience the lows either. I believe that to be true. So if, on the one hand, I have not experienced the joys of marriage, I have also not had a man around to tell me what to do or how to do it. I have no children to make me happy and proud, but I also have no children to distress me and make me weep.

A great-uncle once said to me, "Ida, there are a lot of things in this life that are worse than not being married." I concur. And at the top of that list for me would be "unhappily married." Many a day, after having listened to a new unhappy story in the life of a friend or an acquaintance, I have come home and thanked the Lord for my single blessedness. Within the walls of my own home at least are peace and tranquility. My home is a quiet, restful haven from the world, and that is more than many folks have.

Each of us came to earth with different interests, talents, and missions to perform. The Lord blessed us with free agency, and, upon baptism, gave us the gift of a personal revelator, the Holy Ghost. I have seen that the Holy Ghost may give varying answers to similar questions posed by different people. Often we think that one answer—like one sock—will fit everyone's question, and then we try to force ourselves, as well as others, into the proverbial Procrustean bed, ignoring the ill fit and the personal revelation.

President Marion G. Romney said, "Independence and self-reliance are critical keys to our spiritual growth." ("The *Celestial* Nature of Self-Reliance," First Presidency Message, *Ensign*, June 1984, p. 5.) For us as women, single or married, that independence and self-reliance are crucial to our spiritual maturity and well being. One-third of the women of the Church are single, and all women have a strong likelihood of spending a considerable number of years alone. As women we need to be prepared to take care of our own emotional, spiritual, and financial needs. It may be difficult to face the statistical realities, but I believe we are unwise to ignore them. Fifty percent of Latter-day Saint women in this country will reach age fifty in a first intact marriage. This statistic indicates that the remaining women either will never marry or will be widowed, divorced, or remarried. The chances of a woman's being divorced are between 40 and 50 percent, and for those currently in their thirties, 60 percent. Men tend to marry younger women, and women outlive men by an average of eight years. Married women, therefore, have an excellent chance of being widowed, some for lengthy periods of time. Eighty-five percent of the currently widowed people in this country are women.

Sister Camilla Kimball said at the Paris Area Conference: "I would hope that every girl and woman here has the desire and ambition to qualify in two vocations—that of homemaking, and that of preparing to earn a living outside the home, if and when the occasion requires. An unmarried woman is always happier if she has a vocation in which she can be socially of service and financially independent. . . . Any married woman may become a widow without warning. Property may vanish as readily as a husband may die. Thus, any woman may be under the necessity of earning her living and helping to support dependent children. If she has been trained for the duties and emergencies of life which may come to her, she will be much happier and have a greater sense of security." ("A Woman's Preparation," *Ensign*, Mar. 1977, p. 59.)

In this country, for every one hundred active single women over thirty in the Church, there are only nineteen active men. Adult women greatly outnumber adult men. Plainly and simply, there are not enough men for every woman to have a husband. If I had decided to wait for marriage to make me whole, I would still be waiting.

Had I known in my twenties that I would still be single in my fifties, I might have slashed my wrists. But by my fifties I have learned that I am placed in situations where I need to learn particular lessons. The Lord has individualized education plans for each of us, and for some, that education plan may very well include being single.

When the Lord said, "Come, follow me," I believe he was speaking to me. He went further, inviting us all to become as he is, to acquire his characteristics, to become part of his family, indeed, to go so far as to take upon ourselves his name. His life, his reactions to those around him, his treatment of his friends—male and female—are guidelines for our own behavior. We are all in varying stages of progress in trying to become like him.

When in this process I come into contact with others who, like me, still have a long way to go in their progression to become like him, I try not to let myself become discouraged or to blame the doctrine—or the Church as a whole—for the individual blind spots and inadequacies of some of its members.

Wholeness must come from within, not from without. Marriage does not cause a person to be whole. Single women have a wonderful opportunity to work at achieving that wholeness. If we understand our doctrine, we know that marriage is not a matter of *if* but of *when*. The Lord does not require us to settle for second best. We are half a person only if that is what we choose to be. I do not envision myself as half a person, as someone who will be whole only when I belong to someone else. And I certainly have no intention of ever marrying half a man!

I have often been asked the question, "Hasn't it been a big disappointment not to have had children?" My feelings on this subject are very different from those of many of my friends who have yearned to have children. Some of them have gone ahead as single parents and adopted children. Contrary to prevailing attitudes and practices, marriage, in my thinking, comes before children. Since I have never been married, the question of having children has never been important, significant, or an option for me.

Marriage for me is more important than "being married." I look back at men I could have married when pressures to marry were really great, and with 20/20 hindsight I am grateful I did not. Since I view marriage as a very long-term contract, I view simply "being married" as a very distant second to marrying the right person. I stress this distinction because of the large number of young women I have seen who quickly marry the one in hand out of fear that no one else will ask them. They fear being an old maid, or they fear having no one to support them, or they marry because everyone else in the dorm is. Some divorced women remarry so that the children will have a live-in father or so that there will be a provider in the home. Some older single women panic at the thought of spending old age alone and are not choosy about whom they marry. Such reasons may be sufficient for some, but I have chosen a different course. I would want to know that my husband and I were right for each other and to know that the Lord concurred in our decision to marry.

I think of myself as a woman, a human being, first, and then as a person who happens also to be single. I have found people who feel I have no right to be really happy as a single woman, and although I would not pretend I have always been wildly happy about the Lord's timetable for me (that is, marriage perhaps not until the Millennium), I do believe the promise that if I live the best I can, I will become eligible to receive all of our Father's blessings. Those blessings will include an eternal companion, perfectly matched to me. I would rather have that to look forward to in the hereafter than to settle for second best here just to have a Mrs. in front of my name.

I remember President J. Reuben Clark hoping in his last years that he could endure to the end. Barring accident, I will probably live to be very old, and enduring to the end seems a long way away. I remember standing next to my mother at her dresser mirror and hearing her exclaim in horror at how old she thought she looked. When we did things together, she felt she was more like my sister than my mother, and after having been with me all day, she was shocked to look in the mirror and see an "old lady."

I understand the feeling. I have the same reaction when I have been with my nieces or the young women in the Brigham Young University ward where I serve as adviser to the Relief Society. I look in the mirror and marvel at how the face can be growing so old when the spirit does not feel it. It is hard not to become depressed by the little voice that says, "You're getting old, and no man in the world is interested in a woman as old as you are," because I know, statistically, that the little voice speaks the truth.

I don't envision the scenario becoming easier as I grow older. Seeing the movie *It's a Wonderful Life* once a year is not a bad idea. The circumstance of having no one in your home every day to help you with an unbiased view of yourself and your worth requires some deliberate evaluation of self. I must constantly remind myself that it is what I am, not what I do, that will make a significant contribution to family, church, and community. As I look at others who have been important in my life, the effect has been made because of the relationship. Whether that person was a doctor, lawyer, engineer, secretary, or full-time homemaker is not as important as the relationship I had with that person. Did my friend care? Did my friend give freely of his or her time? Was my friend loving? Was I?

As we mature and grow older, the questions we ask ourselves change. When we are young we might ask:

Am I honest, or do I pretend to be weak or less intelligent and capable—in short, pretend to be something other than what I am—in order to "catch" a husband? I said no early in my life to that pretense. The price was higher than I was willing to pay.

Am I willing to compromise intellectual or spiritual standards to experience marriage on this earth, or do I prefer to wait for the best person for me, even if that means putting off marriage until the Millennium? My own response is apparent.

Is marrying an outstanding man outside of the Church a viable option for me? I would have to follow the Spirit very carefully on that one because I am not sure of the answer. Some men may later join the Church, and some may not. I do know that it takes considerable courage to follow the Spirit when its promptings go contrary to the prevailing rain forest in which we live. I do know also that I would not want to be married to a man who does not want me to become the best that I can be and who does not want me to be an equal partner with him in our home.

President Kimball stated in his address to women in 1979: "Be assured, too, that all faithful sisters, who, through no fault of their own, do not have the privilege during their second estate of being sealed to a worthy man will have that blessing in eternity. On occasions when you ache for that acceptance and affection which belong to family life on earth, please know that our Father in Heaven is aware of your anguish, and that one day He will bless you beyond your capacity to express.

"Sometimes to be tested and proved requires that we be temporarily deprived—but righteous women and men will one day receive all—think of it, sisters—all that our Father has. It is not only worth waiting for; it is worth living for.

"Meanwhile, one does not need to be married or a mother in order to keep the first and second great commandments—those of loving God and our fellowmen—on which Jesus said hang all the law and all the prophets." ("Righteous Women," p. 103.)

Our Heavenly Mother and Father created our spirit bodies, and we lived for an indeterminate period of time in premortality, before coming to earth. We progressed at different rates then, just as we do now. Some perhaps waited there as some wait here. The second major stage of our creation took place when our earthly parents provided bodies for our spirits. Because of the gift of agency we ourselves are the architects of the third and final phase of our creation. It is we ourselves who individually determine what we will be and where we will go, either by design or by default.

If many of us who are single could see the future from the present, I can't help but believe we would start doing some things differently now. We would cease to sit and wait. We would conscientiously develop our talents more. We might change from "job" to "career"; we might get more formal schooling. We would exercise our gift of agency and become comfortable with it. We would not fear to take charge of our lives nor wait to be told what to do by other human beings. We would become responsible for the consequences of our own decisions.

In my fifties I am still trying to decide what to be "when I grow up," and I have recently started a doctoral program. I feel best about myself when I am learning new things and feel that I am growing. The greatest gift I can give to others is the gift of my own well-being. I cannot give from an empty vessel, whether the gift needed be emotional, spiritual, or financial. My gift to God and to my fellow beings is to be who I am and to take upon me the Lord's family characteristics. As I achieve that, I am reluctant to accept someone else's answers rather than to ask for my own, as did Nephi. I rely more completely on the Spirit. And when answers come to me that direct me outside the boundaries of the rain forests—as such an answer directed Nephi when he was directed to slay Laban—I need Nephi's kind of courage and trust in the Lord in order to follow my own script rather than that written by another.

I believe that as I gain an eternal perspective of myself and try to see the end from the beginning, I will use the gospel of Jesus Christ as a ruler for my thoughts and actions and will become less concerned about "what the Church is doing for me."

The question I must constantly ask myself is: Am I willing to pay the price here, whatever that may be, in order to be where I want to be hereafter? Determining and then paying that price is one of the most challenging, heartrending, uplifting, creative endeavors that I—or any of us, single or married—will ever undertake.

Happily Hereafter

Blythe Darlyn Thatcher

As a child I loved the story of Cinderella. I especially loved the part when ordinary, impoverished Cinderella magically became beautiful. I believed the effect was basically universal: The once-plain little girls of the world in due time would, like Cinderella, be transformed into lovely, willowy, young ladies. Knowing I wasn't beautiful or slender yet, I waited patiently for the years to bring that magic.

One fall, coming back to high school, I saw Carol McGowan and Elaine Rogozenski, two girls I had known since grade school, one tall and gangly, the other short and pudgy. Both, obviously visited by the fairy godmother, were suddenly lovely, graceful, and slender. I wasn't disheartened; I just assumed it might take a little longer for my own transformation.

The years have since brought many transformations to me but never quite the Cinderella effect. I am passing fair and sometimes strikingly attractive, but lovely, graceful, and slender I have never been. I blame my genetic makeup: What's a fairy godmother to do with Grandmother's stout English genes, anyway?

Blythe Darlyn Thatcher is a resource department chairman in the public schools. She completed her master of education and educational specialist degrees at Brigham Young University and has done postgraduate work at Utah State University and the University of Utah. She has served the Church as a curriculum writer and in teaching and leadership positions in Relief Society and Young Women.

The Cinderella effect was only one of several major notions I had about what occurs in a girl's life. I also assumed that sooner or later I would decide on a profession, work for a time, get married, settle down to a house, learn to cook, and love reading Pooh stories to my four boys and two girls before tucking them in at night. Now, sixteen years of teaching later and staring age forty straight in the face—single—I entertain different notions.

I was resistant, but I finally had to concede that there would be no fairy godmother in my life. What was even harder to admit was that I would likely never be lovely, graceful, or slender. I would have to make do with passing fair, erratic grace, and elusive slenderness.

I reluctantly relinquished my childish belief in a fairy godmother, but I have known all along there is a God. My childlike faith in God long preceded my wish for a fairy godmother. From my earliest days I was nurtured by my parents' belief and trust in God and Jesus Christ. As a fledgling in Presbyterian Sunday School, I treasured a growing collection of poster pictures of Jesus I earned by memorizing passages of scripture. I loved the flavor of those rich biblical words, and I basked in the affinity I felt with heaven in knowing them.

In those early childhood days I wondered how God took care of everything. I understood his need for angels with so many people on earth to shepherd. Keeping track of sins, I surmised, was done by putting a big black check mark next to the sinner's name. Once people had twelve checks, they would have to go to hell when they died. By the time I was nine, I already had about seven check marks, and I was worried. Adolescence added innumerable check marks to my name, and I gave up that notion in self-defense.

My fifteenth year brought me to the Church and ended my teenaged spiritual decline. I felt cleansed in body and spirit as I was lifted out of the waters of baptism. My sense of affinity with the spiritual was renewed; my faith took on new dimensions.

At sixteen, with anticipation and quiet anxiety, I received my patriarchal blessing. Because life had not always been tender with me, I just wasn't sure that this blessing was going to be all good news. For instance, in my pre-Mormon days I had decided I didn't ever want to marry. Now I wanted marriage with all my heart, and because it counted so much, I feared that, innately, I wasn't worthy. This blessing would be the telling of it. I wanted so much to be celestial material and was afraid my best was only third-level terrestrial. Not only did my patriarchal blessing calm my worst fears but it also provided illuminating insight to my celestial heritage and potential. That blessing has provided continuous motivation to live my life to merit its fulfillment.

As I conformed my life to gospel teachings after my baptism, I assumed my righteous life-style would enhance my marriage possibilities. The "1 chance in 300—or is it 3,000? or 3,000,000?—of marrying an active LDS man" statistics weren't available in those days. I certainly planned to marry, though the process itself was vague to me; there were already thriving cherubs and a happy hearth as I envisioned my marriage.

Since high school graduation, I have never had any five-year plan that didn't have marriage on the agenda. I still don't. There have even been times when marriage was the only substantial item. Nevertheless, one thing the years have clearly taught me is that *marrying* is not the issue; marrying *right* is. For me, that knowing has nothing to do with being too choosy or living single too long. Many factors play on my decision to marry, but the one who ultimately wins my hand will be that man whose direction matches my deepest eternal direction and whose living portrays that commitment. Short of that, I prefer to be single.

Don't misunderstand me. The same spirit that longs for exaltation has immense longing for eternal companionship. It is precisely because I most desire eternal companionship that I am willing to be alone all of this life, if necessary, rather than forfeit my divine eternity. But I would also be ecstatic if, without further delay, that noble companion's advent occurred in my life. Thus far, however, there is no sign of my nobleman on the horizon. And "thus far" has now been some twenty years! It took varying portions of those twenty years for me to, first, recognize my circumstance of singleness and, second, effectively respond.

Sometime in my twenties, I determined that I didn't care when I got married as long as I was married by thirty. When thirty came and went, the reality of singleness began to set in. I thought perhaps I should increase my involvement and "seek for the companionship of one of the noble sons of our Father in Heaven" a little more directly. I began taking community school classes, not solely for that purpose but with the conscious thought that he might be there learning French or creative writing. When I didn't find him there, I thought I would find him on higher educational ground. Graduate school was the answer. Along with the master's degree would come credentials for public school administration—I was looking to my professional career, just in case. He didn't enroll in my master's program, but I still thought the university might be his most plausible setting. So I enrolled in another graduate program. I came away with more credentials and another degree but no husband.

During those graduate school years, however, I did become engaged to a man I met elsewhere. On that engagement testing ground, as in no time before, my long-held perspectives concerning what was right for me in marriage were soundly tested and ultimately spiritually validated. He was not my nobleman, but that then-wrenching relationship now provides me great peace of mind as I continue as a single woman in a world where marriage reigns supreme.

But in those years, even in my twenties, as year after year went by and I remained single, I began to doubt my worthiness for marriage. I searched deep within myself, trying to find what was wrong with me that kept me single. Yes, I could be thinner, prettier, more mature, more spiritual, more intelligent, more ad infinitum. But fatter, uglier, sillier, and duller women than I were getting married.

I did have opportunities—if that's the appropriate terminology for men who would have married me. Ah, but too many Irving Stone romances, and one of my own, had pierced my heart. For me, it has ever been imperative that there be fire, electricity, a camaraderie of personalities and spirits, that the two of us, man and woman, be bondable spirit and body.

My youthful perception of Church doctrine has also held sway. Already believing Christ my Redeemer, the other and lasting appeal of the gospel for me has been that I, even I, through Christ, could eventually become perfect. I have known since my first days in the Church that I am already terrestrial material; I could marry any of several men and ensure myself a terrestrial eternity. That frightens me. For me, it is imperative that the one I marry have my desire for eventual exaltation.

It may well be that my imperatives keep me single, but the very core of me could never enter marriage under lesser circumstances. In no way do I view myself above men; only, for me to marry, that inner equality must be there. Then, in full trust and as one, we could finish working out our salvation and exaltation.

While these perspectives regarding my marriage are the result of much contemplation and introspection, events of the last several years literally forced me to reevaluate and, in some basic ways, to realign my beliefs and my approach to life. The engagement and another wrenching relationship wherein I temporarily lost my sense of self-worth and eternal direction combined with a near-fatal fall requiring extensive recuperation proved sufficient catalyst.

I was still reeling emotionally from both of those difficult relationships when I suffered the fall. I had been four years in graduate school requiring two of my summers while working full-time throughout. I was exhausted and had set my heart on a footloose, rejuvenating summer that was only days away.

It wasn't to be that kind of summer. My fall resulted in a serious concussion, two head gashes, jammed neck and shoulder muscles, a broken left wrist, multiple bone bruises, and a right knee with a partially torn ligament and damaged kneecap. To have so many physical injuries and at the same time be suffering such intense pain of mind and spirit, and then to find that after a month of constant pain and swelling it was necessary that I undergo knee surgery—it seemed more than I could bear. The accident was the last straw after so many months of awfulness. I was sorely disappointed to have yet to be alive, and I bitterly agonized my complaint to the Lord.

I spent hours in that torment of soul as I thrashed on my bed with my cast and brace and pain. But after those hours, I began to reason. As I contemplated all the reasons why the fall should have killed me, it also began to dawn on me how rather miraculous it was that not only was I not dead but I was not paralyzed, permanently crippled, or subject to seizures or blackouts. And somewhere in that abyss, I also became aware of my agency. That day despair began to be replaced with life-saving resolve.

I determined that if I *had* to live on—and since I apparently was supposed to—I could not continue in my spiritual posture. Of all my afflictions, I knew that most in need of healing was my spirit. Finding myself at such a low juncture, I realized that, however unwittingly, *I* had allowed my circumstances and my impressions of good people in better circumstances to make me feel I had no right to expect exaltation for myself. That was a revelation to me. Extending such power to others and believing such false intimations about myself had nearly cost me my exaltation. I understood about the "arm of flesh" in a way I had never understood before.

That life had appeared so hopeless when my doubting replaced my faith made it apparent how much truly believing meant to me. Through the years, as I learned gospel truths and principles, I had worked diligently with myself to get rid of the self-ascribed, spiritually damning innuendos left over from my early years—suspecting that I was somehow an exception to Christ's redemptive powers, particularly toward exaltation; suspecting that the sins I had committed or been victim of made me an unsuitable candidate for eventual godhood; suspecting that there was a nontraversable chasm between people of eternal potential and me. I had wanted to eradicate those monumental doubts from my life entirely, but for all my efforts they had gone only as far as the back burner of my mind. Through all my years they had inconsistently, but gnawingly, come back to haunt me. I had tried to ignore them, hoping they would eventually give up or die out. I realized I was now staring them straight in the face. They would finally really have to go.

It was all too clear to me what doubting the effects of my righteous efforts and doubting the Lord's promises to me produced. "All things produce after their own kind: the offspring of faith *is* faith, the offspring of disbelief *is* disbelief." (Joseph Fielding McConkie, *Seeking the Spirit* [Salt Lake City: Deseret Book Co., 1978], p. 11; italics added.) I had given disbelief space, allowed it to increase, and in my recent, darker days, even fed it. I had nearly sold my soul for it. That I had so nearly succumbed intensely sharpened my sense of the dichotomy involved.

Faith, beyond the gift, and agency became verbs, not concepts. I resolved: If I have a choice, which I do, then I choose to have faith—faith in the Lord, in the Atonement, in prayer, in repentance, in forgiveness, in service, in my potential, and in the goodness and potential of others for exaltation; faith in the scriptural fact that the Lord does not make status exceptions about who may share in his blessings but all people "are privileged the one like unto the other, and none are forbidden." (2 Nephi 26:28); faith that the Holy Ghost, keeper of all truth, can witness and imprint on my soul my worth, an imprint that with nurturing can withstand all false assessments—and I choose to nurture; faith that as I rely on the Lord through exercised faith, I am capable of overcoming all barriers, self-imposed or otherwise; faith that in my process of perfection, I can eventually attain all the attributes of godliness.

I am a daughter of a *Heavenly* Father. I can "reasonably expect to become like [him]." (Henry B. Eyring, *Excellence* [Salt Lake City: Deseret Book Co., 1984], p. 20.) I had not realized before how dependent that expectation is upon my exercised faith. Constant nurturing is an essential that I had not previously understood or fully employed. I now recognized it as the practical complement to knowledge and faith.

In the past I had had difficulty letting go of my trespasses, even some minor ones. I somehow felt a sort of humility in their remembrance; I also felt a persistent sort of futility in my righteous reachings. Truly exercising my faith in Christ, I began to see that repentance and forgiveness afforded me a reconciliation with Christ and my Heavenly Father that I had never before allowed. I let go of those trespasses, the misconstrued humility, and the persistent futility. I decided to actually trust in the sacrifice and promise of the Lord.

With new perspective I understood that this life is to prepare me to meet God and become like him. It was understood by all concerned that as I grappled with life I would commit my share of sins. What I have learned about myself is that once I really understand what is right to do, I usually persist in the right. It is to my eternal benefit to forgive myself for sins I have repented of, sins that I committed not because I clearly desired to do evil but because I did not perceive clearly the benefits of righteousness. As I repent, the Lord offers me forgiveness, a forgiveness that is consecrated as I take the sacrament each week. The Lord in his perfection is able to forgive me; I do him honor to complement his forgiveness of me with my own. I also further my progression, aligning myself consistently closer to godhood.

These spiritual insights did not occur in an instant, but there is that moment forever cut out of time when I decided to doubt no longer. And then I decided to exercise faith consistently. That has made all the difference.

The acid test of how well I could overcome doubt was Mother's Day, 1986. Locking my door as I left for church that sunshiny Sabbath, I thought, If we have to celebrate Mother's Day, this is a good day to do it. I was happy with life and thought I could handle my lack of brood as we celebrated that accomplishment by other women.

Through Relief Society and Sunday School I was outside myself, enjoying my learning and appreciating the efforts to ensure our ward mothers a happy day. Tender memories and feelings for my own ever-kind and benevolent mother enhanced my appreciation for her and for those women in my midst.

Sacrament meeting began with a musical Primary tribute to the mothers. Afterward, two of those Primary children chose to sit with me, one on each side, and I busied myself giving them paper and pen to occupy the moments that might lag for them.

"Would all the mothers please stand? We want to give each of you a cookbook for Mother's Day."

I had known the request was coming; I thought I was prepared for it. Why, then, was there this sudden heart-wide pain, depleting me of strength and spirit? I felt desolate; the two children beside me only heightened my sense of isolation—and it had nothing to do with not getting a cookbook.

I knew what was wrong; I was still vulnerable. I will never be past wanting husband, children—to belong in that fashion. I was quick to realize, though, as I sat through the remainder of the meeting, that I had a choice. I could suffer my anguish all the day long, or I could exercise my faith to get back outside of myself. I primed my mind and heart to have me be a blessing to all with whom I came in contact for the rest of that day.

After church I took a short nap to help renew my strength and spirit. Then I made arrangements with a couple to care for their children while they went on a trip. I went to a Mother's Day dinner for my mother-by-affection (my parents are long deceased). After the dinner, I took home my dear eighty-nine-year-old grandma-by-affection. I also had a gentle, meaningful conversation with a treasured but downcast friend.

When I returned home that evening, I was completely refreshed, with no hint of my earlier mourning. It did not escape me that I had been a genuine blessing to several people that day, and one of the reasons I could offer my time and heart in that fashion was that I was single. Another, more significant, reason was that I chose that day to trust in the Lord's timetable for me, and I exercised my faith in that to the benefit of others. That day has remained a convincing reminder that faith is power, divine power, healing power, and it is mine.

Truly believing in Christ and his promises and consistently endeavoring to match my thinking and actions to that faith—it is this, I have finally learned, that not only sustains me but empowers me. Possessing the gospel is not at all sufficient; I must, with consistent accuracy, apply the gospel and make the power of its principles mine. That may sound like common knowledge, but it has been the hardest-won, farthest-reaching scholarship of my life.

What I have explained has taken me all of my almost-forty years to learn. I have learned it all as a single woman. Perhaps I would have learned it sooner in the security of marriage; perhaps it would have taken me still longer with a husband and children bolstering my sense of security. No matter. I do know it was imperative I learn; I am keenly aware of the eternal implications.

Having thus learned, I find that my enjoyment in living life has been greatly enhanced. Turning forty single doesn't cast a first cloud on my happiness. In fact, I have big plans to celebrate this benchmark birthday. Engraved invitations will be sent to the surely thousands of friends who, over the years, have invited me to their wedding showers, trousseau teas, wedding breakfasts, wedding receptions, and wedding parties. Since this birthday is on an August Saturday, an over-the-hill birthday open house for this still-single woman is in the works!

I have always figured I missed out on a good thing by not having a wedding shower or reception to get me going in life. I've worn out most of the things I used in my first twenty years of adult life, so engraved on the invitation will be the option (preferred!) to bring a nonwedding gift. At the open house I will make sure an embossed receipt is given for each beautiful, elaborate, and lavish gift that comes through my door. Then if, in the not-too-distant future, I get married, those guests need only bring their receipt to my wedding reception. I'm sure all my friends will think this a delightful crossing for me into middle age.

As I have journeyed toward this fortieth year, I have made do with passing fairness, erratic grace, and very elusive slenderness. But while my outward comeliness has remained basically unchanged, with divine tutelage and blessings quantum leaps have occurred within. All who know me long and well would attest to my ever-increasing inner beauty and refinement. Better yet, I have come to realize that this manifest beauty which is mine is a rare, everlasting loveliness.

I still love the story of Cinderella, and I still wish I could be lovely, graceful, and slender in appearance. Not for one moment, though, would I trade transitory outward beauty for this internal, eternal comeliness, not even for a moment.

"Whence Cometh My Help"

Christine Timothy

I was standing at the counter picking out a shirt and tie for my dad's birthday. I knew I wanted a light blue shirt and a classy-looking, red, patterned tie, not too heavy on the pattern. The clerk came over, and, having found the items I wanted, I placed them on the counter. He said, "Oh, you are brave. Most women wouldn't pick out a tie for their husband. They're afraid he won't like it, I guess."

Before I knew it my response was, "Well, this is for my father, and he wears anything I buy him." The clerk, suddenly embarrassed, muttered through the rest of the transaction. All I really meant was that my father loves me, and he would wear a green and purple suit coat if I gave it to him. There it was, however, the crux of the purpose of life as we now know it. Woman is to be with man and . . . well, you catch my drift.

Most of the time I don't think about my being single. I'm usually too busy on the job, out shopping, or involved in some project or other. There are the rest of my waking hours, however, when the thought does cross my mind—like the moments

---

Christine Timothy is a special education teacher in the public schools. A licensed speech pathologist, she earned her bachelor of science and master of science degrees in speech pathology and audiology from the University of Utah. She has had leading roles in many opera and musical comedy productions and has been a member of the Mormon Tabernacle Choir. She has served as the Primary music leader in her stake and the chorister in her ward's Relief Society.

when I am all alone for dinner or for a good tear-jerking television rerun, or I have two tickets to the game at the university and I can't find anyone available to go with me, or when I am at church. It is at church I feel most obviously single, because being married is such a vital part of what I know to be true concerning my eternal salvation. I guess the bottom line is that I do think about being single, maybe more often than I had originally thought.

The person who looks back at me in the mirror every morning does so with love and understanding. This is possible because of what I have included in my life and because of the character I have developed in living each day the best I know how. (Some people may say *character* is right!) Admonished constantly to "love yourself so that others may love you," I try to do that a day at a time, although some days are harder than others. It's like the saying "You are beautiful, but some days you are just more beautiful than others."

One approach that helps me to love myself and live my days well is establishing projects and completing them. I find joy in seeing the results of a project finished. Sometimes I expend tremendous effort in completing a project. I am aware of a parallel here: the happy end of my life is going to take that same kind of effort and it will yield a commensurate joy. My projects certainly help, but my faith, my friends, and my family are what I most rely on to maintain my ability to love myself, to be loved, and to develop inner strength and character.

I remember one fall day when I was about nine years old. I was swinging in our backyard, back and forth, up and down. Each time my feet touched the ground, I'd push to keep the momentum going. I loved to sing, so while I was swinging I started singing, "Oh, it is wonderful that he should care for me / Enough to die for me! / Oh, it is wonderful, wonderful to me!" I kept singing this over and over until several hours had passed, and I had found the rest of the words to "I Stand All Amazed." (*Hymns of The Church of Jesus Christ of Latter-day Saints*, 1985, no. 193.) It must have been at this time in my life that I began to realize a testimony, no longer blind faith but a testimony, from within my own heart and mind.

I have often talked about my Beehive class as an example of building my own character. There were thirteen girls in that class with 100 percent attendance but with no real sisterhood.

Competition was fierce in my ward among the young women, each one trying to prove herself. I was right there with the best of them, proving away.

I was one of the lucky ones—I could sing. Everyone knew it, and I was asked all the time to sing in church. So when it came time for the ward Spring Sing, and every class was asked to participate, I thought for sure I would get to be the star of our class presentation. Our teacher, dear Sister Boyer, came up with the idea of a wax museum where each girl could come to life and thus display her talent. I thought this was a stupid idea because I had some grand number in mind where I would be the soloist and the other girls would be the Andrews Sisters in the background, or something like that.

I did get to sing one solo, so I at least felt an important part of the whole production. And that's exactly what Sister Boyer was trying to teach us—that even though we were all talented individuals, we still needed each other to be happy. I don't remember winning any awards for "Madame Boyer's Wax Museum," but I know I began loving everyone in my class for the sister each was individually as well as for how each girl fit into the picture of my life.

This may have been the time in my life when I found out that we all need each other. Married people need me in their lives, and I need them as I need my single friends. If we learn to appreciate each other for the talents we have to give, marital status becomes much less a divider and oftentimes brings us closer together. After all, each one of us is an individual child of our Father in Heaven, and learning to stand on your own as a person is something that must be done, married or single. My character has been strengthened by developing my talents according to this pattern.

Many people assume that since I am past a certain age and not married, there must be something wrong with me. "You are too picky" is what I'm often told. I've even had people accuse me of not wanting to be married bad enough. To them I say, "That's just exactly what it would be if I had that attitude—bad enough!" How can I forget the many nights I participated in singles activities where innumerable other young women and I vied for the attention of the limited number of eligible priesthood holders in attendance. Now those were some character-building opportunities.

Remembering the church singles dances always churns something up inside me. I know those very dances have been successful for many in their search for an eternal mate; however, I just never had any experience close to that while I was attending them. One dance in particular, my last, was truly an evening to write about in my journal.

I had just purchased a darling outfit and my hair looked perfect that night. You know how sometimes it just goes where it should? Anyway, even if I do say so myself, I looked smashing.

There are certain strategies to the circulation game at singles dances. That night I pulled out all the stops and tried every strategy I knew, starting with keep moving and don't stay with a pack of girls. That night I even talked to five or six different men. One was a single high councilor in our stake. We stood and talked for about ten or fifteen minutes, but I guess it never dawned on him the music was for dancing, because he excused himself politely and left me standing there holding up the wall. Just then a voice came over the loudspeaker and said, "All right, girls, it's your turn. Go and get 'em!" I just stood there for a minute, watching other girls grab a partner. I thought to myself, I have been here for two and a half hours, and not one of " 'em" has asked me to dance. I suddenly felt disgust or despair, I don't know which, but I do remember heading straight for the door and driving home in tears.

This experience was not the most inspiring one, but it gave me a basis to build upon for dealing with future disappointments of equal proportions. Life has its Goliaths that we must all learn to deal with. There have been many in my past, and I'm sure there are still more to come, but in following David's example, relying on faith, I know I can rise above them.

I've had the opportunity to write, direct, or star in many Mormon musicals, but there is one that has had a surprising effect upon me. From the first time *Five* was pulled together to the most recent time it was performed, I have found a strange comfort and solace in its script and music. In addition to that, I have found friendships with the cast that have buoyed me up and sustained me.

The story is about five girls who are growing up together. We see them first at a slumber party discussing what they expect from their lives. Then we see them years later when their lives have unfolded. These girls didn't all get what they dreamed about during the slumber party: each life took its own course.

In this musical I see my friends. I see real-life faces with real-life situations like those in the story. I see my life. The truth is my life has not turned out like I thought it would at my slumber parties, either. I'm not the only single woman with this realization, but I have found comfort in the message of this musical that I am not alone, that there is someone who loves me and blesses my life by answering my prayers.

I have found that qualities my parents possess of patience and unconditional love give me great strength. Whether married or single, I need to develop these and other qualities to bring me closer to my better self. My lot seems to have been to have the influence of family members who have understood my singleness not as a detriment but as a part of my progression in this life. I am convinced that through my parents' example I have unconsciously adopted many of their qualities because I value what they are, and I have tried to emulate their life-style. Granted, it is a little different alone, but it is no less important nor is it impossible.

Being single is a challenge. Facing life one day at a time is a challenge. Continually building character is a challenge. With all those challenges, I have a choice to make: either I can go through this life being happy, knowing that my Heavenly Father knows my individual needs; or I can be miserable, by shutting out his influence in my life. I have found that with my faith, my friends, and my family I can find the way to make my journey a much happier one. I can draw from them the strength to do whatever I find is expected of me. Without them I cannot.

From Seeds to Roots and Onward to a Tree

Shelley Swain

She asks, "Do you like to write?" "Not really," I reply. She persists, "Would you like to write one chapter for a book about single women in the Church and share your ideas?" Even though writing is not one of my strongest skills, I am tempted beyond control at the chance to share my single woman's views. My mouth says yes before my good sense can stop it. Now as I sit with pen in hand, I find the words don't come easily. I'm trying to share very, very deep feelings that are well protected. I remember the words from a favorite book by Beryl Markham that "silence is never so impenetrable as when the whisper of steel on paper strives to pierce it." And so I feel now as I strive here to share my ideas. I can't do it. I stop.

It's months later, and I begin again. I'm flying in a 737 jet-liner now and am looking at the bluish-white cauliflower below me. It's easier to stare at this never-ending scene than to put my ideas into writing. I'm returning from a marvelous experience in Boston and Washington, D.C. It has left me with a zest for life and with the feeling that life should be lived fully and richly. Where do these ideas come from? Why do I feel this way? How can I hang onto this feeling long after the trip has faded into my

---

Shelley Swain is the personnel director of a regional retailing organization. She earned her bachelor of arts degree in political science from the University of Utah and is enrolled in the executive master of public administration program at Brigham Young University. She has served the Church in numerous callings, including that of ward Relief Society president.

dreams? I remember that Belle S. Spafford said, "A woman's reach is bounded only by what her mind accepts and her heart allows." I am continually discovering that my happiness or sadness depends upon the beliefs in my heart and mind because these ideas determine how I interpret my daily experiences. That is why I can be in the same situation as another and yet have a much different experience. Yes, it's my beliefs that will allow me to hang onto the feelings produced by the experiences I've just had.

I look out the airplane window and see a patchwork of greens, browns, and pieces of modern society connected by roads. Maybe I can share pieces of my world that connect me to my present philosophies. I have a plan for my chapter now—I feel encouraged in this experiment. I look out the window again and see hundreds of homes and hear that we are preparing to land in Chicago. My life also has hundreds of experiences, but now I must try to sort out only a few to illustrate my views. The easiest place to start to try to understand is probably at the beginning.

I'm in the air again, soaring for home and remembering home as a child. I remember with a smile bringing home insects and frogs and my mother remarking that she was more concerned about checking my pockets before I came into the house than checking my two younger brothers'. It seems like I spent half my time doing what the boys did and half my time doing what the girls did. I was a skinny, red-headed, freckle-faced, tall, budding ballerina liking kick ball, mountain climbing, and collecting insects.

My brothers and I did the same household chores and were expected to do well in all subjects in school. When I showed no interest in sewing or cooking, no one seemed to notice. Once in junior high school I called my mother at work when I was sick at home and asked her how to fix a can of soup. She laughed and told me to just read the can. Even then she didn't start a great campaign to teach me how to cook so I'd be prepared for the future. She knew she'd taught me to be responsible and that I would learn that skill on my own at the appropriate time. Common sense did prevail, and I do cook now. While some other girls' mothers seemed to emphasize homemaking and grooming, my mother paid more attention to my behaving well, being aware of others, and being a good person.

Other children's parents enrolled them in a variety of music, dance, or athletic classes. My interests seemed to be my own and were encouraged only after I had made them known to my parents. Nevertheless, my parents constantly introduced my brothers and me to many aspects of life, such as ballet, opera, exotic foods, different cultures, the great outdoors, and on and on. They wanted us to be aware of the world around and beyond us. From this vast array, I was able to make my choices.

My father expected me to do my share of the work and to take care of myself. I was supposed to act like a lady but not be a wimp. I tried to act like many other girls, to be flirtatious and dependent, but I wasn't very successful. I felt insincere and silly, and it showed. No one in my home acted this way, and I really didn't see the need to act differently from the way my family acted. I was competitive with my brothers and found that we each had our own strengths and weaknesses. I translated this thinking to the girls and boys around me. I didn't believe that boys could do certain things better than I could or that they had to have certain interests because they were boys; my family life proved different. Apparently that is a fairly liberal idea, which is most amusing. My family didn't try to be liberal; we just thought we were being practical.

My present notions about male and female relationships are quite egalitarian. I trace the awareness of these feelings to a particular experience. When I was in junior high school, a friend's older college brother took the two of us bowling and then dropped her off first when we returned home. She and I had been practicing our flirting with him, but it was just in jest, and we thought that he knew it. Instead of taking me home, he took me to a nearby canyon road and tried to kiss me. His advance seemed wrong, and it scared me. I didn't know how to get out of the situation gracefully but I knew I wanted out, so I promptly jumped from the car and started to walk home. His jaw dropped. I guess he thought that because he was a college boy I would be putty in his hands. I thought he might be trying to take advantage of me, and I just didn't want him to have his way.

He drove alongside me as I continued to march home. I realized I had gained control of the situation through the element of surprise, so when he finally convinced me that he would take me right home, I got in the car, and he whisked me to safety. He told me that I had brought this all upon myself and that I should learn my lesson.

I felt he was wrong and went to my father for counsel. My father said that my flirting might have given the wrong impression but that this older person also had the responsibility to take my age into consideration and to act appropriately. My father then went over to the boy's house and talked to the boy. That was a powerful experience for me because my father reassured me that I needed to take an active role in my relationships with men. He taught me that I should expect good treatment from men because I was worth it.

My mother did several things that had a strong effect on my thinking. She never intimated that my self-worth was dependent upon a man; if anything, she indicated that it was completely independent of others. If I didn't have a date to a big school dance, I was told that I was fine and that my other interests and activities were just as important to my becoming wonderful. She taught that people develop socially and in other ways at different rates and emphasized that I should not worry about it.

Another important aspect of my years at home was my involvement with ballet. It grew from watching my first Ballet West *Nutcracker* performance at age six with my father into a passionate goal to dance professionally. As a result, I filled my teen years with activities very different from those of other teenagers. I either danced or taught dance every spare moment. I can still recreate in my mind my battle with gravity as I sought to soar, balance, move, and twirl as I wished. My body remembers the feeling of the lengthening of a muscle in a stretch, the power as I leapt or moved quickly, and the moment of weightlessness as I turned on one toe or balanced perfectly for a few beats. My heart will always yearn for the freedom of beautiful steps combined into exhilarating continuous movement blended perfectly with music when skill allows the soul to be expressed fully. Ballet is endlessly trying and straining for a lovely motion—sweating, groaning, failing, aching, growing tired, and going on with the hope of conquering. And gently one day the motion is yours. The control over the new step comes and goes but is there more often. And then on to the next earth-defying and even lovelier ambition. I can't write about ballet adequately, but all my cells remember and tingle at the thought of it. I now watch great ballet intensely, shutting out everything around me and reliving the stirrings in my veins so deeply that I feel an encompassing joy and am usually moved to tears.

In ballet I learned to be disciplined, competitive, independent, and tenacious and to reach for beauty. I wasn't trying to be magazine-cover beautiful, but in ballet I was trying to create beauty and so became beautiful. I had to dig deeper into my heart to have the courage to face the seemingly impossible ballet movements than to choose the right mascara and lipstick. I learned to shoot for high goals and pursue them with all my energy. It was so wonderful to be that excited about life and to look forward to every new day because of the joy I would find in dancing. I have a very hard time now not wanting to live life as passionately as I did during the ten years of joy I spent in pursuing my dream of dancing professionally.

The love of ballet helped me overcome my fear of having different goals and interests than other girls my age had. It broadened my view of the world. I learned to love all the arts and to search out for the best the world could offer. My interests grew wider and deeper while the views of some I knew narrowed as they sought only to get married. My interests continue to grow, and I continue to strive for a life filled with richness. I'm not easily content with mediocre because of my learning to strive for perfection in ballet.

College was also a significant shaper of many of my present views and decisions. I was a ballet major for two years and danced exhilaratingly, eight hours a day, six days a week. During this time I learned that several physical limitations due to skeletal structure would not allow me to continue into professional dance. I experienced a great loss of passion and joy for the next five or six years as I tried to replace ballet with all sorts of other activities. I became very vulnerable to cultural ideas of what gives a woman her worth—physical beauty, marriageability, and ability to bear children. It took many years of analyzing, anger, and reassurances to overcome these silly beliefs. But I learned a very important lesson: even if you give everything you've got to achieve a goal, you may still not achieve it. Life isn't always fair, and you can't always make your dreams come true in the way that you may want. The loss of my goal to dance professionally at first made me afraid of trying again and of failing. I chose safer goals, risked little, and lived less brilliantly. But after years of not attaining the goals of marriage, children, or career I finally threw away my timidity and realized that to fail is not unbearable, just unpleasant. I began to risk and work hard again, and I have made great strides in achieving my career and school goals. I finally realized that through my unfulfilled ballet hope I had learned that it is important to try because you become so much more in going through the process.

I switched to political science, hoping to do exciting work overseas. In my political science classes I learned to question and analyze events, causes, and ideologies. I learned to be unafraid to explore ideas and to analyze my thoughts and the thoughts of others. I remember my first political science class. The class was almost all men, and it dealt critically with political issues in this country. We had to write a research paper on an issue that interested us. I wrote about the role of the press in the balancing of power in the government. When the top three papers were chosen to be presented orally to the class, mine was one of them. I was surprised and delighted. The professor wanted me to polish the paper and submit it for publication. This encouragement reaffirmed my belief that I was just as capable as others in the class and that I had something to offer.

I learned in college that my success was determined by me. My grades depended upon my ability to think rather than upon my marital status, my looks, or my sex. I liked that because I could be successful and could control my success in that environment. I was responsible. I learned to do whatever seemed very difficult or unnerving. I learned to look for truth and to apply it in my life. As a result, I was no longer content with limited views of myself or others, nor did I accept judgment or advice about my destiny without critical review and contemplation.

With my newfound joy in reading and exploring ideas, I came across many ideas that continue to enrich my perspective. Henry David Thoreau impressed me with his ideas in *Walden*. He strips away all the nonessentials of life and makes a mockery of them. He tries to get at the essence of life, where true joy is found. He points to the basics in living, solitude, joy of your own company, and the grandeur of nature. I find myself going back from time to time and rereading parts of *Walden* to shake myself up, to see where my heart is set and how taken in I am by the nonessentials and the cultural follies of this life. I also look to see how sluggish I've become in my thinking, and then I am provoked to move forward. These gymnastics keep me from dwelling on what I haven't got and cause me to set goals to grow and live productively.

The joy of learning led me to look at others' lives for enlarged perspective. Corrie Ten Boom taught me about how much effect a single woman can have if she is possessed of a strong moral fiber and if this fiber is built from daily doing service, praying, and reading the scriptures. She has lived a full, happy, and rich life despite never marrying or having children and despite experiencing the horrors of a World War II prison camp. She has influenced many lives significantly by sharing her love and testimony of God.

Another influence has been Lowell Bennion, who opened my eyes to the difference between saying what you believe and doing what you believe. He stresses being actively involved in life rather than safely watching it go by. He encourages us to test the Lord's teachings by doing them and thus allowing the refinement to come through experience. When I read his writings, I don't want life to pass me by. I at least want to try.

One other person who has contributed heavily to my perspective is Carlisle Hunsaker, an institute teacher. From him I learned that I need to continually look at and develop my life philosophy because it is from those thoughts that my actions will spring. For example, do I believe that people are basically good or bad, and thus how do I respond to the commandment to love God, myself, and others? When I review my life philosophy, I can then determine my commitment to the gospel and where I need to progress.

The Savior and his teachings have shaped my perspective and play a continually greater role in my daily life. I love the story of the Savior telling Martha that Mary has chosen the good part by listening to his teachings rather than being too concerned about functions in the house. My role as a woman, a daughter of God, is to develop into a celestial being, not simply to pursue getting married. My being married or the righteousness of my husband does not guarantee my development into a disciple of Christ. I cannot find in any of the Savior's teachings the many ideas that are perpetuated in past and present cultural expectations of women. Many of these ideas confine women to the kitchen, limiting them; the Savior's ideals do not limit a woman's potential. I have limitless potential; I want limitless development. The more I ponder this spiritual perspective in contrast to mundane and worldly perspectives, the more I experience peace in my heart and a confirmation that my perspective is pleasing to our Savior. I also am more able to deal with the frustrations that I sometimes experience when confronted by others who ask why I want to go to graduate school and only hope that I'll get married soon. I have hope for the things I desire and faith in the goodness of the Father's plan for me. Reading the scriptures, daily prayer, and daily striving to treat others as I should helps me keep this perspective and feel a peacefulness in my soul. I am here to live each day as well as I can by loving the Lord, obeying the commandments, and learning to think and live by the truths of the gospel. All other aspects in life are just that, aspects of this life. What is more important, whether I can cook or whether I can love those around me? Of course, we need skills to survive in this world, but I think we often overemphasize those skills until they become more important than our life philosophy.

The Savior was perfect, and that in itself separated him from those around him. I think he understands very well the challenges of this life and of living a singular life. His teachings answer all of the concerns of those who are not encompassed by the typical family unit. I know that I alone must account to the Lord for my life's actions. This view helps me to live and direct my life in a productive and satisfying manner. The temple reinforces the truth that individually we must account to the Lord, and that reinforces the eternal perspective in my daily experiences. The purpose of the temple ceremony is to learn of Christ and to covenant to do the Father's will. As I go through this ceremony, focusing on these purposes, I am challenged, uplifted, and renewed in my purpose and my understanding of this life's experiences. I can laugh at, ignore, or fight against cultural limitations with renewed energy. The Savior spent his time performing his life mission, not trying to be a part of mainstream society. I am comforted when I spend more of my time trying to become a disciple of Christ rather than trying to fit into the "norms" that surround me.

In studying the gospel I have learned to try to distinguish between what is cultural and what is doctrine in what I read or hear. I've worked very hard at eliminating many learned cultural notions about myself as a woman, about what determines my success, and about how I should conduct my life. I've used reasoning, talked endlessly with others in my situation, and then contemplated the scriptures. The scriptures are a source of clarification for me, but I realize there are some problems with how women are portrayed in them. I see, however, how women progressed in those cultures despite those conditions. The four Gospels are especially guiding and comforting to me as a single woman. The Savior's reverence for women, men, and children is equal, even though the specific references to women in the scriptures may be vague or negative because of the culture that surrounded the writers and translators. As I read the scriptures, I feel the words of the gospel piercing my heart and know that they are meant as fully for me as they are for anyone else.

Being single, of course, does have its concerns. One of my frustrations is not knowing whether I'll be married. Consequently I must continually devote some of my time to pursuing this elusive goal. I've wrestled with how much energy and faith to exert in the righteous desire for marriage. I've seen too many men and women consumed by wanting to get married and thus becoming miserably unhappy and self-absorbed. Moderation and balance are necessary in my pursuit of finding a partner. This approach has evened out the peaks and valleys of my feelings about wanting and needing love in my life. I have also finally realized that married people are not perfect, that I don't need to be perfect to get married, and that marriage is probably more a matter of what I expect from another and of the timing of meeting someone fairly compatible to me. My self-worth is not dependent upon my marriageability or my physical beauty, as society would have me believe. Rather, I believe my self-worth is based only on my divinity as a child of God.

Another concern is that I'm afraid of living alone. I'm a very social creature; I tried living alone but I didn't like it. I get tired of playing musical roommates as well as friendships, but it's better than living alone, at least for now. I worry about isolation the older I get because I'll fit less and less into mainstream society. Those in my circumstances will scatter and become harder to find for friendship. Another aspect of this loneliness is a lack of physical warmth. It would be nice to have someone's arms around me and be told how much I'm loved.

But along with that love will come the challenges in that relationship.

I realize that these same concerns of isolation and loneliness can also be experienced in marriage. If I enjoy each friendship as it happens day by day and learn to love others, then I can do something about isolation and loneliness and keep from becoming their victim. My friendships with my family and with others provide comfort, reassurance, companionship, and joy now.

Another concern of mine is the possibility of never having a child of my own. I anticipate greater sorrow as I get nearer to the end of my child-bearing years. Because of changes in society, however, I may adopt a child and still experience the joys and challenges of child-rearing. I have already experienced many more earthly blessings and opportunities in life than many of the people on the earth—and on top of that I have the gospel. Life isn't easy for anyone, even if it appears so. Life certainly isn't always fair, either, and I find strength in making myself come to grips with my set of trials and setbacks. We all have to deal with disappointments and deep sorrows. The more I force myself to deal with the issues in my heart, the more of these issues I resolve and thus the more freedom I give myself to enjoy life. Part of that process is that I continually make and remake life goals. I don't want to get to the end of my life and realize that I've just marked time. There is much good to be done in the world and having a family and raising children is not the only worthwhile thing to be done. I can love and assist others all the time in many ways that can be very fulfilling.

It is a strength to enjoy your own company rather than always to rely on others to give you joy. Although I do not want to live alone, one helpful skill that I am continuing to learn is the skill of enjoying my own company. I'm learning to enjoy nature, the arts, and education by myself, as well as with others, as another source of strength, joy, and happiness in this life. The joy I can actually experience with others is controlled by me, not by them. I am the only one who can determine how much joy I experience, and that depends on how I manage my perceptions of what is real and what is good. When it sometimes seems that others have all the material, spiritual, and emotional joys of life and I wonder, "Why can't I or why don't I have what it takes to be successful in society?" I feel that I'm wasting my energy to be so consumed with what others have that I don't have or with how unfair the world is. The world just is unfair, and the quicker I accept that, the quicker I can get on with pushing myself to reach my own potential. As I strive for that potential, I act from a positive and strong base that gives me the strength to love and serve. And love and service are the major purposes I am to accomplish in this earth experience.

I've landed in Salt Lake now and have returned to my irregular-by-choice routine affairs. It's after hours at the office, and I am feverishly trying to finish this chapter. It took the deadline of tomorrow to push me through the last walls that hide precious beliefs. The one thing that I or anyone can really hang onto in this life is the Lord and the gospel. To tap into this strength I have learned not to counsel the Lord but to listen for guidance and direction and to enjoy the companionship of the Spirit. I am then directed to push onward, focusing on my goal of living according to gospel teachings through whatever I encounter. The Spirit also gives me courage and perspective so that I can have an abundant life even though there is ugliness, sadness, and chaos. I am beginning to understand that the Lord is the life-giving and sustaining element and that the Atonement is available to me. I am so overwhelmed at these gifts alone that my heart is filled with gratitude to the Lord rather than with complaints or despair. Of course, I must work continually to maintain this perspective. I am so thankful for the many blessings I have that I feel uncomfortable spending my time without enjoying them or being immobilized through discontent. There are times to mourn, but the length of those times needs to be managed. The joy I allow myself to feel, the depth and strength I realize by dealing with trials, and the desire to grow is congruent with the purpose of this life, and the Spirit speaks confirmation to my heart as I focus my energies in this direction.

Sojourn

Mary Ellen Edmunds

I graduated from Primary in the Rock Church near the post office. The woman who was assigned to give The Talk spoke to us about "you sweet young girls on the threshhold of womanhood." Afterward I sat with my friends, and we tried to understand the significance of this passage into MIA, but we were still much into kick-the-can, bikes, snow forts, marbles, playing in our tree house, and watching the Lombardi brothers dig tunnels in the field next to the hospital. Nevertheless, we went to MIA. We each had a bandlo that we glued plastic things on, and I still remember how long it took me to make my felt daffodil to put on the top. We sat through lessons on the steps about achieving a temple marriage and a happy home and family. "If you do THIS, then THIS will happen."

Things haven't quite turned out the way my MIA teachers indicated they would. The Rock Church is still there, but the hospital is in a new location, the Lombardi brothers moved who knows where, the bandlo is in a box in the basement, my friends are scattered in many places, I'm approaching fifty, and I live alone.

Mary Ellen Edmunds is an associate director of training at the Church's Missionary Training Center in Provo, Utah. Formerly a member of the nursing faculty at Brigham Young University and the director of an international program for children in Nigeria, she served three full-time missions for the Church in the Southern Far East Mission, the Philippines, and Indonesia. She has also been a member of the Relief Society General Board.

Some of the situations and milestones of being single have been hard. I had a rough time with the knowledge that I was reaching the age where I likely would never bear a child. It was a very difficult reality for me. I had always looked forward to having my own children and anticipated having several.

There have been adjustments related to living alone, and there are questions at times like, "Do you mean to tell me that I'm going to need to do all these things for myself?" There's so much I don't know, and it has never been easy to ask for help from others.

It isn't always comfortable to go places alone, either, even to Church meetings. I'm very aware of those who have family to sit with, particularly of women who have husbands. There is also a variety of responses to me from others.

There have been times during interviews with priesthood leaders where I have felt even they weren't sure what to ask or how to listen and instead have filled in their time with me talking about their families and situations. That has been a cause of frustration. I've not had regular visits from either visiting or home teachers. Visiting teachers have tried, but from the time I returned from a mission in Indonesia in 1978, I have not had home teachers. I have requested them but have not had a visit, and I found it uncomfortable to keep requesting. I likely would have felt more need to follow up on my requests if I didn't have my family—my parents and brothers and sisters, many of whom live near—and wonderful neighbors. It hasn't been that I have always needed something fixed or done—although that does happen—but I wanted someone to know something about me and have some awareness of my circumstances, needs, strengths, and interests.

I've been faced with the awkwardness some feel when they find out I'm not married. The question that leads to this realization is usually something like, "What is your maiden name?" or "How many children do you have?" I respond with, "I'm not married." No tears, no embarrassment, just the fact: I'm not married. But so often the response, especially in body language and tone of voice, indicates that I'm to be pitied and surely I'm missing all the things that bring true happiness in this life. Others sometimes even convey to me that they think I'm only pretending to be happy, that I can't really be happy as a woman (with or without children) without being married.

There are many who try to make something happen. They line me up with their son or their brother or their neighbor or a nice single man they used to know who's close to retirement. "You could go on a whole bunch of missions together." There have been some enjoyable experiences, and there have been some disasters. I have never responded well to the feeling I have sometimes, "So this is what it has come to—leftovers." No doubt there have been some men who have responded that way to me, too. Then there are the well-meaning souls who say, "Oh, I just know you'll marry a General Authority some day!" or "I just know there's a special man being saved for you!" For me, or from me? The message usually comes across this way: "*Some*day you'll be happy, I just know it."

There have been many times when I've watched my brothers and sisters and friends with their families and have had a very difficult time. Some of those little children have seemed like kindred spirits, and I have wondered if they are like my own children would have been if I had been able to have any. I've had times in my life when I've wondered about the rest of my patriarchal blessing because of the promises about children and family that have yet to come. Such instances turn out to be times of searching, pleading, pondering, and stretching. *Am* I happy? Fulfilled? Peaceful? Progressing? Achieving? Does anything I have accomplished in my life count in the whole scheme of things? Are we only "on hold" while we're single? Does the *real* living only happen with husband-wife combinations?

I recognize that there are things I could not have done had I been married, with or without children. I don't pretend to know how significant these experiences are in an eternal sense, but I am convinced that they matter. I have many relationships that are eternal in nature. I have consciously decided I will give my days and years the best I can and trust in a loving, wise God to help me know what I need to know, and do what I am supposed to do, and become the best MEE (Mary Ellen Edmunds) possible.

Several years ago, probably close to twenty years, I became aware that I spent a lot of time thinking—and worrying—about what I *didn't* have. All around me were reminders of what others had that I didn't. It wasn't so much their possessions as their situation—their home and family and children. During this time I read a little story that had a powerful effect on me. I don't remember just where I found it, but I'll never forget how it made me feel and the deep impression it left:

Two little children were put early to bed on a winter's night, for the fire had gone out, and the cold was pouring in at the many cracks of their frail shanty. The mother strove to eke out the scantiness of the bed covering by placing clean boards over the children. A pair of bright eyes shone out from under a board, and just before it was hushed in slumber a sweet voice said, "Mother, how nice this is. How I pity the poor people who don't have any boards to cover their children with this cold night."

This little story stopped me in my tracks. I thought about it over and over again, coming to the realization that I had spent far too much time in my life thinking of all I didn't have instead of all I did have. Here was a little unknown child who taught me a great lesson: she was grateful for present blessings. She was looking at everything from the perspective of what she had. And thus was born my personal theory of relativity.

I know there will always be many people who have much, much more than I do—more time, more clothes, more talent, more hair, more pets, more toys, more children, more things—but there will also always be millions who have much, much less than I do, and in many situations much, much less than they need. I began to understand it is not what I have, but what I enjoy, that brings real happiness. My theory of relativity ties in with such hymns as "Count Your Blessings." (*Hymns of The Church of Jesus Christ of Latter-day Saints*, 1985, no. 241.) I have been making a conscious effort to expect less and appreciate more. This change is making a noticeable difference in my life. It's a process, not an event, so it takes time, but I feel progress, and I am enjoying the effort.

I have spent a total of six years living and working in developing countries, most of the time as a missionary. I have had many powerful learning moments, and I have had some magnificent teachers. But there has been a price to pay for this education and experience. I remember how hard it was for me to say yes to a call to serve in Indonesia. I was thirty-six years old and had not been home three years from my previous mission. I felt like I was just beginning to become established somewhat in my life. I was becoming aware of things such as building up toward retirement and learning to take care of myself. I didn't know if I could handle another mission physically or emotionally. But within hours, particularly during some time in the Provo Temple, I knew that this was the right thing for me to do—certainly not the easy thing, and not what I would have chosen without prayer and the process of ask, seek, and knock.

In Indonesia I spent about a month in Jakarta with the mission president and his family and my companion, a young woman from Malaysia. Then we were given our assignment: we were to live and work in central Java in the city of Solo. We arrived there after an all-night train ride and found our little home. I was surprised to find it so rough. No sinks and no toilet, just a hole in the floor. The well where we'd get most of our water had fish and junk in it. The large open storage tanks where we'd store what water we could get from taps were lined with scum. There were rats, cockroaches, scorpions, flies, mosquitoes. I kept saying to myself, "Self, you have done this before; you can do it again. Shape up; get tough; hang in there." But I felt discouraged, and I knew that this was going to be a difficult adjustment.

That night I was awakened because I hurt and I couldn't breathe. I had anticipated that—my previous missions had been in humid areas, too, and I always had asthma. I used my inhaler, but it was a while before I could breathe comfortably. Meanwhile the mosquito and bedbug bites hurt and itched. I was hot and sweaty. I lay there on my back looking up, imagining I could see beyond the ceiling, and cried unto the Lord. I complained, "Why was I sent here? What is going on? Is this supposed to be a good experience? Am I being tested again? I don't want to go through all of this again, I just don't. I like to breathe!" I'm sure I mentioned all of the things I could think of that I didn't have in that situation. I was beginning to feel like one of the great martyrs of all time.

The next morning I decided to begin cleaning and organizing. One thing I had noticed was that my fan was filthy. I had a little three-speed fan that worked sometimes; it depended on what else was running in our neighborhood. The power fluctuated in an amazing way. We already knew, for example, that by 6:00 P.M. our one light in our living area would be gone—too much competition. Time for the candles again. But I did have a fan, and I took it out by our well to clean it.

I was just starting to take it apart when a woman came to the door, which was near our well, and asked if she could get some water. I had noticed her before and felt happy we had something to share. I noticed, too, that she had the same dress on as before, that she had several children, and that she was pleasant. She began to talk to me while she was drawing water. She wasn't complaining, but she told me some things about her life. Her husband, a polygamist, seldom visited, and she was having a struggle trying to care for her children. She lived behind us in a makeshift dwelling that had no electricity, no water, and not even a hole for a toilet. Something began to happen to me while I listened to her, the woman at the well, as I became more aware of my three-speed fan. My theory of relativity was brought powerfully to my mind and heart on that important day in December 1976, and this good woman was my teacher.

A few weeks later some Church members who lived in a Chinese cemetery as squatters invited us to visit them. We rode our bikes in their direction, and they were waiting for us on the main dirt road to show us how to reach their homes. In one home the man, Sukiman, had built a small bench for us to sit on. We talked for a while, and then I asked a typical question, "How many children do you have?"

Some special, unspoken communication passed between him and his wife, and then he responded, "There is no one following us." It wasn't just, "We have no children." In the Indonesian language it was more like, "There is no posterity." He added, "We have had children, but we didn't know how to care for them, and they all died." That hurt. That didn't seem fair, not when so many of us knew so much about caring for children and had so many resources to help us.

We kept talking. At one point Sukiman asked, "Sister, do the members of the Church in other parts of the world pray for me?"

I knew that some did, even though I hadn't always been among them, and I responded, "Yes, Sukiman, there are many members who pray for you."

He became emotional and said so sincerely, "Isn't that wonderful? I pray for them, too."

This was in 1977, and we were receiving letters from home about the shortage of water. It was a year when there wasn't enough snow and rain, and everyone was concerned. Church members would ask us, "What do you hear from your family?" We told them about the water shortage, and they expressed concern.

Things became relative in a powerful way one day when a missionary received a clipping from a newspaper reporting that in a part of California the people were being restricted in their water usage. They had to cut down to only 120 gallons of water per day for everything they needed. 120 gallons! I thought of Sukiman. I wondered what in the world he'd do with 120 gallons of water in one day, even if he could possibly carry that much water from the well, which was quite a distance away from his home. And to think that the 120 gallons would be safe water. . . .

During that month of February we got a message from our mission president in Jakarta informing us that all members of the Church throughout the world were going to fast and pray together, for each other, for all the problems and challenges in the world that members were facing. We were to let the members of our branch know.

We knew that many of the members ate only one meal a day and not because they were fasting. But they responded, and we gathered in our branch meeting on Sunday. One of the brothers was asked to pray, and I'll never forget the feeling I had. At one point I even opened my eyes, so touched and impressed was I with what he was saying. "And please, Heavenly Father, take care of those who are suffering because they don't have enough water. We have plenty. Could You take some of ours and share it with them?" It wouldn't surprise me at all to learn one day that He allowed them to share their water.

In the Philippines in 1973 I was serving as a health missionary, and my companion and I used to take the bus from Manila to Baguio about once a month. We began to notice one little girl who was always at the bus station in Baguio when we'd arrive. She sold peanuts and newspapers. She always had on the same ragged T-shirt, shorts, and thongs. She got so she recognized us and would run to greet us when we'd arrive. One day we took her picture. She looked at the camera curiously, and we wondered if she'd ever had her picture taken before. We took the film back to Manila and got it developed. On our next trip we brought her a picture of herself and could hardly wait to find her.

She came running when she saw us, and I handed her the photograph, expecting her to exclaim with delight that she was happy to have it. But she took it and kept looking at it intently, finally asking, "Who is this?"

I couldn't believe it. Here was a little child who, in the literal sense, didn't know who she was! I said, "It's you."

"Me?" She looked even more closely at the picture.

"Yes, it's you." Then I got an idea and pointed to the hole in her T-shirt. "Do you see this hole? Here it is in the picture. This is your shirt, and this is you."

Then I could see by the look on her face that she had at last discovered it was a picture of her. She dropped the papers and peanuts and went hollering through the bus area, "It's me! It's me! It's me!"

Relatively speaking, I know a lot about myself and my relationship to my Father in Heaven, the Savior, the Holy Ghost, my earthly parents and brothers and sisters, and to everyone I meet. Here was a little girl who knew almost nothing about who she was and who God was. My little friend didn't know that she had kept her first estate and had the potential to return to live with God. It seemed to me that I could learn from that contrast. I could learn of gratitude for knowing who I am and for a chance to help anyone else know more about who they are, especially with regard to their relationship to their Heavenly Father and their purpose for being on this earth with the rest of us.

These and many other experiences helped me realize how much I have and caused me to do a lot of pondering about how much I enjoy what I have and how willing I am to share. My experiences have brought me perspective and help me understand more about myself and others and about life. One thing perspective does is teach me more about why—why I was asked to do certain things at certain times in my life. I have found that for me nothing happens in isolation; it is all connected. Each thing that I have said yes to that was right and good has been tied to other opportunities and experiences. I have called my chapter "Sojourn" because through my experiences I have become so conscious of how brief life is, how temporary and critical.

I find I take more time to try to make sure things are in the right order. First things first, as they say. I can remember reading in Doctrine and Covenants 88:119 about "a house of order." I had always pictured that as a home with "a place for everything and everything in its place." Now I've expanded the picture to include order in the sense of timing and value: the right things in their right place in that sense. I am peaceful about timing and seasons, knowing that indeed, "to every thing there is a season, and a time to every purpose under the heaven." (Ecclesiastes 3:1.) I want to do the right things in the right order. I know that this life *is* the time "to prepare to meet God" (Alma 34:32), as Amulek taught, and that although there are some things I can't do as a single person, there are things I can do because I'm single.

Occasionally there are times when I feel down, frustrated, discouraged, or overwhelmed. I thought of an idea about twelve years ago that helps me put things in perspective and keep them there. I decided to schedule time to be depressed. During the day if I begin feeling a bit low, I remind myself that I have a time in my schedule for that and I can wait. Then when it's time, I really get into it. I have to be in a place where I can't be distracted by anything too positive or cheerful. That means if I'm around people, I let them know that for a few minutes (I try to make ten minutes the absolute maximum) I'm going to be depressed and they should leave me alone. Sitting in a corner is a good location because there's less chance of spotting a book I want to read or catching some happy scene out the window. This approach has helped me by causing me to see more clearly that I have far more to be happy about than sad. I usually end up spending less time being depressed than I had planned, and sometimes I start laughing or become motivated to do something productive, interesting, enjoyable, and uplifting.

I love having things to look forward to—a holiday, a book I'm going to read, something I'm going to do with or for someone. I love looking forward to things that are an hour away, a day away, a year away, or more. I love learning new things. A friend of mine, Florence Richards, decided that each year she would learn something new. I remember that one year it was learning to play the accordion. I admire her plan and have tried it. Recent things I've tackled are learning (finally) something about computers and learning American Sign Language, because it's one of my responsibilities at the Missionary Training Center.

I have worked to genuinely enjoy others' success and happiness. There were times in my life when I felt some envy for what others had that I didn't have, but through consciously working on it I have learned what a good feeling it is to be genuinely happy with others. And I realize that I have opportunities and happiness that others may share, too. Sometimes I've had people say to me, "You're so lucky to be where you are, doing what you're doing." I don't know what part luck may have played, but I have done many things in my life because I knew they were right for me to do, although they have been anything but easy. When God has asked me to do something hard, I have decided he must know I can do it.

Sometimes, in implementing my theory of relativity, I handle my frustrations by going outside myself. My office has a window, and I pretend I'm standing out there looking in. It's an interesting exercise to look in on my situation and life and experiences. Some of the positive thoughts that come when I "step outside" include realizing I am free and have choices and opportunities. Then I might remember walking with a young boy in Indonesia as he poured out his heart about his hopes and dreams, his yearnings. The reality of his situation was that he might never reach some of his goals. As we walked that day, my young friend asked me why. We talked about what we do with what we have. I told him my feelings about the scriptures that mention "according to that a man hath" and my consciousness that in many respects many of my brothers and sisters in temporally-challenging situations were doing more with their challenges and opportunities than I with mine. He had worked and saved for about five years to serve a mission, and he valued his two years highly because he had worked hard for them. So much of what he and others invest their time and work in is that which they can take with them. So much of what I have is of the world.

Once while I was living in Nigeria, West Africa, I became very sick. I was trying not to be discouraged about it, but those old questions kept coming, questions that usually began, "Why . . . ?" I had received several priesthood blessings, and it was hard not to doubt my faith or my worthiness to be healed.

I kept wondering what I was accomplishing because I was so sick every day and any exertion only made matters worse.

It was Christmas time in 1984, and we held a program in our branch. During the course of the program I picked up a little child named Blessing. I could tell she wasn't feeling well, either. I held her in my arms and looked at her and began to communicate with her. It wasn't words—I didn't know her language and she didn't know mine—but it was a powerful sense of communication. I wondered about her in my heart. "Little Blessing, what is life like for you? Do you have any hope at all? It must be hard to be hungry so often. And to have sores on your feet." I knew I could have no real understanding of what that little child was feeling, but our eyes locked and neither of us looked away for a long, long time. I realized I was crying. I don't know that I would have had as much sensitivity for how she was feeling if I had enjoyed perfect health while I was there.

Eventually I was sent home because of illness and spent three months of "crash and burn," physically and emotionally. I had never been a quitter before. There were too many unanswered questions at once. Too much wondering about why. And the majority of the questions had to do with "Why me?" Not so much why did I get sick while I was there so that I couldn't finish, but why was I the one who was taken away and given special care in a modern hospital in America? Oh, I can think of all the things that people would usually say if I tried to explore that question with them. But I was thinking of Blessing and my other friends there who were also not feeling well and who struggled every day with pain and sickness. Why MEE? Even now, I haven't quite settled that question in my mind or my heart.

I was able to go back for a couple of weeks in April 1985. It helped me feel somewhat more peaceful about things. I attended Church in the same branch, and it was good to see my friends. One little soul whom I nicknamed Broomstick was there. I called her that because she was seven years old and weighed twenty-three pounds. I used to scoop her up and take her to the front of our small chapel with me; I'd find her just inside the door, seeming not to have the energy to go any further. I loved holding her and the other children. I loved the way they held on tight and soaked up the love. I know they could feel how much they were loved.

On this particular Sunday in April, near Easter, I picked up my tiny friend, Broomstick, and held her. We sang "I Know That My Redeemer Lives" (*Hymns*, 1985, no. 136) that day. I felt a prompting to sing it to her, so I did. "I know that your Redeemer lives. . . . " Some of the phrases were particularly powerful and touching. "He lives to bless you with his love." "He lives your hungry soul to feed. He lives to bless in time of need." "He lives to hear your soul's complaint." "He lives to silence all your fears. He lives to wipe away your tears." I found I couldn't sing after just a few phrases; I could only whisper the words to her. She was watching me, and I wondered if her soul could understand what I was trying to share. "He lives, our kind, wise, heavenly Friend. He lives and loves you to the end." "He lives and grants us daily breath. He lives, and you shall conquer death." It was an unforgettable experience.

My theory of relativity is tied closely to all such experiences. I think of those who have less than they need and look at myself with so much, much more than I need of many things. I have decided that an important attribute of being godlike is described in Doctrine and Covenants 104:17: "For the earth is full, and there is enough and to spare." I spend a lot of time pondering this. Enough *is* enough. Why is it sometimes so hard for me to have enough—and to spare? If only we could properly see others' needs in light of our own wants. (See Spencer W. Kimball, "The Gospel in Action," *Ensign*, Nov. 1977, p. 77.) Oh yes, if only I could do that more. For me, I have realized that when I spend a lot of time thinking about what I don't have, I miss all the chances to be content and happy with what I do have—the "clean boards" to cover myself with on a cold night. A friend said, "You can never get enough of what you don't need, because what you don't need never satisfies you." Amen.

In 1981 I had the opportunity of spending a short time observing work being done by welfare services missionaries in a refugee camp near Bangkok, Thailand. Here I learned other permanent, powerful lessons. One afternoon we visited with a family who had fixed up a nice home in the space they had been given. As we were visiting, I noticed that a little girl bumped into a small bag of rice. It spilled all over. Immediately, without any anger, the adults and children stopped what they were doing and helped pick up every single kernel of rice. I watched that simple act, and I learned much from it about the value of even a single kernel of rice. I thought of how much I must have wasted during my life that likely would have been of great value to someone else.

Another time at the refugee camp I noticed a little girl watching me. She had on an oversized pink shirt. Every time I'd try to look directly at her to smile or communicate in some way, she'd run away. I wondered about her, who she was and what she'd had to experience at her tender age. Toward the end of the day we went back to the place where the missionaries had their office. I sat near the window with my back to the outside. My arms were stretched out, and my hand was on the edge of the window.

After a while I noticed the little girl in the pink shirt approaching me, walking very quietly, watching to see if I'd turn around. I didn't. I decided just to sit quietly and see what happened. She got closer and closer. When she was right next to me she stopped, and we were both very quiet. I didn't turn. Then she reached up and touched me, and ran. It was like electricity, that quick touch from a tiny finger. I felt it deep in my soul and was moved to tears. I sat there thinking and feeling when I noticed that she was coming back. I still didn't turn but waited to see what would happen. Again she approached carefully and quietly, and again she stood waiting. Once again she touched me and ran, and I felt another deep and powerful response. She did this another time, and still I didn't turn. The last time she did this she stood as before but then reached up and put her whole small hand on top of mine and pressed it hard. I wept. I felt so much love for that little child and kept thinking, "Oh, little child, who are you? Where are you from? Are your parents alive? Do you have any brothers and sisters? Are there people who care about you and are helping you? Where will you go? Where will you live?"

Later as I thought about the little girl in the pink shirt, I found myself thinking about my theory of relativity. I had been blessed constantly and abundantly in my life; my own needs were far better met than this child's. I realized anew that there was so much good I could do if I would be willing. I could bless and nurture others and help assure blessing and nurturing in others' lives. "As thy days may demand, so thy succor shall be." ("How Firm a Foundation," *Hymns*, 1985, no. 85.) I have felt that so strongly in my own life. God knows me. Every single day. He knows my needs. I'd like to be more that way with others.

What seems critical to me, then, is not whether I am married or single, but that I am striving towards being perfect: whole, complete, and pure, prepared for what God has in mind for me. It's as King Benjamin described when he invited us to become as little children:

"For the natural man is an enemy to God, and has been from the fall of Adam, and will be, forever and ever, unless he yields to the enticings of the Holy Spirit, and putteth off the natural man and becometh a saint through the atonement of Christ the Lord, and becometh as a child, *submissive*, meek, humble, patient, full of love, willing to *submit to all things which the Lord seeth fit to inflict upon him*, even as a child doth submit to his father." (Mosiah 3:19; italics added.)

I probably have resisted and whined and moaned too much and haven't been what anyone would call submissive. But I'm trying. It's extremely important for me to know that I am doing the will of God. I need to know in my heart that what I am doing pleases him and helps him in his work. I feel a tremendous peace from knowing that.

One thing that has helped me very much through all the ups and downs of all the years of my life has been the knowledge that God lives and that I can communicate with him any time. Prayer has been such a significant source of help, comfort, peace, and direction. I like to pray specifically, to think, ponder, and listen. It means a lot to me when there's time to spend an hour or so and have a real dialogue rather than a monologue. I like to take notes sometimes when I pray, writing down impressions and feelings that come. I have had some marvelous experiences doing this. I remember when I was having a particularly difficult experience in my life trying to find the light at the end of the tunnel. I was praying and got a feeling to take notes. What I wrote down still has a lot of meaning and significance for me. Writing in my journal or writing letters to friends also is a great help in sharing my feelings and ponderings.

I gain a lot of enjoyment from the scriptures, and I find it makes a difference if I'm reading and studying every day. I purchased some scriptures on tapes, and I listen to them when I am driving by myself. It's good to use another sense, and I discover, in hearing, some different emphasis or meaning in a particular verse or section. I also love the hymns and find the words very meaningful. If I have an experience in which a hymn is particularly powerful, I like to write that down. Then I can go back in my journal and remember that day or that experience in which the hymn taught me something. I also like to cross-reference the hymns in my hymnbook, adding scripture references to those already listed in the new hymnbook. I like to underline, too, the words or phrases that have special meaning to me.

I am deeply grateful for the privilege of attending the temple. The blessings of being in that holy place increase my peace and fortify me for all that's outside in the world waiting for me. Temple attendance helps me gain perspective, understanding, and insight. I feel spiritually enlightened when I'm there. I love to see friends there; it is one of the best places on earth to run into someone you love. Temples have always seemed like places of refuge and sanctuary to me. I find answers to questions, a lightening of my burdens, and a wonderful sense of comfort while I'm there.

I'm aware of the influence of what I read, see, and listen to upon my thoughts and actions. I work at reading, watching, and listening only to those things that I want to remember, things that will inspire, lift me, and teach me important lessons.

I like to do things that make me stretch and grow, such as choosing to drive a different way to work, mending a misunderstanding, finding a new way to do a routine thing, memorizing something, being the first to say "I'm sorry," and being honest and real with people. In other words, I try not to get caught in a routine or in being predictable, but rather to explore new ways to do the same things and to look for new adventures or opportunities.

Humor has helped me through my life. I have tried to develop a good sense of humor. I found when I was working as a nurse and teaching nursing that there were times when humor could save the day. There were times, too, when situations weren't funny. I have tried to develop a sensitivity to others' feelings and not laugh at their expense. I still have trouble with that at times, laughing at people instead of with them, but I keep working on it. I want to be kind and gentle and never embarrass or make fun of anyone. It hurts me to see someone else hurting. I also don't like to make light of sacred things. But I do believe that we can be happy and cheerful and that life is generally wonderful and a tremendous adventure.

I try to help and lift others through being cheerful. I believe that "men are, that they might have joy." (2 Nephi 2:25.) I think it's healthy to be happy. I want to radiate love, goodness, optimism, and hope in my countenance. I'd like to live so that everyone I meet would know I love them and am genuinely happy because I know that God lives, loves me, and believes in me. I'd like to help others experience this same kind of happiness. I like the way it's phrased in Mosiah 18:20, that we are willing to bear one another's burdens that they may be light. I want to help lift burdens so they can be bearable.

I'm convinced that happiness is possible in almost any situation because I have observed it in such a wide variety of circumstances and have experienced it myself in so many different ways. Happiness is more tied to attitude than to situation, which for me has direct application in my singleness.

One day I attended a funeral that was particularly moving for me, and I wondered about what would or could be said at my own funeral. I have thought about making a video, and I still might do that to share a message with those who might come to my funeral. It's so much fun planning it that even if I never get it done, I'll have enjoyed the experience.

Another idea I had was to write a talk about myself as I'd like to be remembered, and then do my best to live so that someone could give that talk and it would be true. This idea is also tied somewhat to my desire to be like good people I have known in my life, people who live principles and values that I'd like to live in my own life. Once I made a list of ten people besides my family who had had a significant effect on my life. I didn't just list the names but listed some reasons why I felt these particular people had had such an important influence on my life. One thing it did for me was to bring up the question of whom I had influenced—had I had opportunities to help others in such a way that they experienced an increase of hope, direction, optimism, or motivation to do good and be good? I hope so.

Besides those other wonderful people who have had a powerful influence in my life are my family, who are in their own special category. I am so grateful for parents who have allowed me to learn by doing and to find who I am with their constant love and support. It is a blessing to live so close to them and to have the privilege of visiting them almost every day. I am thankful for four brothers and three sisters and their families. I am also aware of the blessing of good friends. I haven't had a great many close friends, but those few have had a significant influence in my life. I've always had wonderful associates in the places I've worked as well.

Life is a magnificent adventure. I'm so happy to be alive! I'm grateful for the progress I'm making in things that are important to me and look forward to learning, understanding, and applying gospel principles more fully as I continue my efforts to learn and grow. I want to explore more about denying myself of all ungodliness. I want to understand the law of consecration better. I want to live the law of the fast more fully, having enough and to share more often. I want to make promises carefully and then keep them. I want to develop increased personal integrity. I want to learn more about what it means to follow a living prophet. I want to increase in patience and gentleness.

I know that things that are now relative must some day be absolute—that I must be absolutely clean, pure, obedient. Meanwhile I try to get better at the process.

A verse in the Doctrine and Covenants impressed me very much. It's in section 88, verse 95: "And there shall be silence in heaven for the space of half an hour." The quality of that silence will likely be different from silence I've experienced on this earth, and I wonder what I will think about during that half hour. What will be important to me then? What is it that will bring peace of soul at that time? In that very silent, final half hour I'll think about the most important things. I'd like to do that better right now, as I look for chances to practice—during the sacrament, during prayer, during other times of pondering and meditation, during scripture study.

Could there be anything more wonderful than the chance to work out our own salvation with the help of God and others? Some have the chance to do that in teams, husband and wife, and others in a wide variety of situations. Whatever the situation, whatever the circumstance, there is the privilege of living principles that bring blessings and of knowing joy and peace and progress in this life.

I am convinced that our Heavenly Father wants us to be happy in this life and in the life to come. I know that his gospel in its fulness has the answers to all my needs and all my questions. He has shared with us all we need to know, to do, and to be in order to be happy. I know that God is alive, aware, and full of understanding and mercy. He is gentle, just, kind, patient, and fair. I am content with that and filled with peace, with bright expectations for my eternal future. And oh, how I hope that "then shall I see his face with pleasure." (Enos 1:27.)

Status: Human Being

Kathryn Luke

Forty-seven and single! Did I plan it that way? What did I do wrong—or what didn't I do right? Wasn't my faith strong enough? Was I too selective? Did I not pray hard enough? Was I too independent? Did my profession get in the way of marriage? Did my mission put me out of touch? Perhaps I shouldn't have gone away to college?

I could spend my lifetime asking such questions and never find an answer. In the process I would be a very unhappy human being, living with what might have been rather than what is. The questions used to weigh on my mind, and I would feel guilty as I wondered if the desires of my heart had been directed appropriately. Now I prefer to ask myself what I can best be doing to make my life meaningful and worthwhile right now, as a single, never-married person.

This attitude may suggest to some that I have given up on the idea of marriage in this life. I have to admit as I approach age fifty that the prospect of marriage lessens. I am promised in my patriarchal blessing that I will have a family, but it doesn't

---

Kathryn Luke is an elementary curriculum specialist in the public schools. She received her bachelor and master of science degrees in elementary education from Brigham Young University and is currently enrolled in a doctoral program at the University of Utah. She has served the Church as a missionary in the Central British Mission and as stake and ward Relief Society president and Young Women president. She has also served as a member of the Young Women General Board.

specify when that blessing will be fulfilled. I believe, however, that the time frame for marriage to a worthy mate extends beyond this lifetime, and so I still have hope.

The marriage relationship can and should be the deepest bond two people can develop, and thus I know I am missing one of the greatest blessings available to us as mortal beings. When I observe a man and a woman who have created a celestial family unit here on earth, my heart is touched, and I yearn for that total commitment and bonding in my life. But I also believe that developing relationships with others is one of the greatest challenges we have, and this challenge is one we face in or out of the marriage covenant. So although total commitment for eternity cannot exist outside the marriage covenant, I can enjoy and nurture many deep and lasting friendships.

I don't really focus much on my singleness unless someone calls my attention to it. I much prefer to consider myself a human being first. That way I can function as a whole person without feeling I am restricted because I don't fit the mold of "married woman." I have been fortunate to live in a ward where my singleness hasn't prevented me from contributing as does any other adult in the ward. Some of my best friends are married couples who are able to forget marital status and include me in their parties, their family gatherings, their circle of friends. As I join in, however, I am constantly reminded by my married friends that this acceptance occurred because I reached out as well. I never felt I was different. I always felt I had something to contribute, and therefore, I was needed.

One of the greatest things a single friend and I did to involve ourselves with ward members was to offer to share with families a slide presentation. We had created it to report a trip we had made that took us to nearly every Mormon historical location from Salt Lake City to the state of Vermont. As a result of that offer, we received so many invitations to participate in family home evenings that it took us over a year to fill all the requests. What a great blessing that was to us as we visited with couples and families. They welcomed us into their homes and hearts, and we drew them into ours.

There was a time when I felt too much emphasis was being placed on the role of woman as wife and mother. I knew too many outstanding single women to believe that no blessings were forthcoming to them just because they were single. I also knew that none of these women had intentionally decided to remain single; marriage had just not been a blessing thus far in their lives. I have now come to realize the Church is perhaps the only institution, religious or secular, that speaks of the importance of the family and the vital roles of wife and mother. That emphasis on these roles in no way lessens my personal worth and my ability to contribute to the building of the kingdom.

I have also learned I can't necessarily change how other people think, but I can control the way I feel and think about myself and others. I am the one who must determine how I will deal with my singleness. I define my value and identity in ways other than that of wife and mother; I know for myself that I am of value for who I am, regardless of my marital status.

As most young children do, I decided at a young age what I wanted to be when I grew up. I wanted to be a secretary. Of course, as a young child, I had little knowledge about what a secretary actually did. My ideas came from watching movies that generally portrayed the exciting, sometimes romantic, side of a secretary's work. So I always dreamed about being a secretary and falling in love with my boss and marrying him.

Pursuing my childhood dream, I enrolled in the commercial track in high school to learn secretarial skills to prepare for the work world. At that time, I had not seriously thought about going to college, so I did not even consider the college preparation track. Although education was encouraged and valued in my family, college was not an expectation. In fact, no one in my immediate family or among my cousins had attended college. Family finances were such that a college education for any of the children would have been very difficult. Besides, I assumed I would work for only a few years until I married, and then I would quit and become a full-time wife and mother.

Sometime during high school I began to receive encouragement from the school counselor and from other important people in my life to think about attending college. My older sister and I began talking about returning to our hometown of Provo, Utah, to attend Brigham Young University together. She deferred going to college and waited a year for me until I graduated from high school. Upon graduation, I immediately found a summer job and saved most of what I earned for college.

The time for attending BYU arrived, and I registered as a business education major. My main purpose in taking business education classes was to increase my skills for working in the business world. I was planning on attending BYU for only one year.

Like so many freshman women, I had hopes of meeting and dating Mr. Right. But as had been the case during high school, my dating was very limited. I did meet a young man who paid special attention to me, and we began dating seriously during the Christmas holiday break, which we both spent with our families in California. He decided to remain in California, but I returned to the Y for the winter quarter. After communicating through letters and telephone calls and visiting in person when he came during April conference, our romance blossomed, and I accepted his ring.

When I completed my freshman year, I returned home to prepare for marriage. As the plans progressed, I began having second thoughts, but I was afraid this opportunity could be my only chance for marriage. I needed to be careful about changing my mind. Even with that concern, however, I became more sure that the engagement should be broken and the ring returned. That was perhaps one of the most difficult decisions I have made, and there were times during the next few years, especially as I remained single, when I questioned my decision. As more years passed, though, I knew I had made the right choice.

When I turned twenty-one, the age for young women to be able to serve a mission had just been lowered to twenty-one. No prospects for marriage seemed near. Since my early teens I had occasionally thought about serving a mission but had never discussed the subject with my bishop. When my bishop called me to serve a full-time mission, I readily accepted. My parents supported my decision when they determined I was serious in my intent. Within six weeks, I had received my call to the Central British Mission and was in the mission home in Salt Lake City. My mission proved to be a turning point in my life, especially in my career goals.

Through my missionary work I found that I enjoyed working with people and that teaching was a very satisfying experience. The daily tracting and the frequent rejection of our message were discouraging, but the few occasions when people accepted the message of the gospel and entered the waters of baptism were thrilling. I experienced the joy of service.

I didn't realize how meaningful my teaching had been until I returned home at the conclusion of my mission and became a secretary again at the same company I had left. I found I was not happy with my work, that the challenge was no longer there, and that I missed teaching and interacting with people in more meaningful ways. Teaching had caught my fancy. So, two years after being released from my mission, I quit my job and returned to BYU as an elementary education major.

Insecurity gripped me as I wondered how I would succeed in my classes after being away from campus for several years. Would I be able to compete with the younger students fresh out of high school? Would I be able to get good grades? As a result of these concerns, I found myself devoting every minute possible to studying and completing assignments. The effort paid off, and I earned straight A's that first year back. Fortunately, I became a little wiser the second year and realized there was more to college life than just studying. Service units provided an avenue for social interaction that was meaningful to me and caused me to reach outside myself.

Because there were more eligible young men in my new environment than there had been in my home ward and stake, I began again to have hopes of meeting and dating a man I would marry. I was now older than many of the students, however, and I watched as the older and more mature young men dated the younger women. I also discovered that being a returned sister missionary was a threat as a potential date for some men.

During this time I met many young women in their mid and late twenties who were very unhappy with their single status. Like me, they had assumed they would be married by that time in their lives, and they felt they couldn't have value without being married. I, too, began to question my self-worth, to wonder what my purpose in life was to be, and to wonder if I was doing something wrong or wasn't doing something I should be doing in order to receive the blessings of marriage and family. I eventually sought a special priesthood blessing, which reassured me of my Father in Heaven's love for me and of his approval of my life to that point. What comfort that blessing gave me, then and even now. I gained a new awareness that it didn't matter whether I was married or single. What really mattered was what I did with my life, whatever the situation in which I found myself. For many women in the Church, perhaps including me, the blessing of an eternal marriage and family will not occur in this life. My challenge is to be patient and develop and use my talents in meaningful ways. I realized that I can contribute to the kingdom and to the community. I can create happiness for myself whether or not I have a husband or children.

After graduating from BYU and receiving my certification to teach, I returned to California where I received a teaching position in my home school district. During my first year of teaching, my principal asked me if I had considered becoming a school principal. I hadn't. She suggested I had the ability for such leadership and encouraged me to think about it. I felt complimented by her suggestion, but at that point, I felt I would likely remain in the classroom as a teacher. I enjoyed teaching fourth-grade students. Besides, I never thought I would teach for too many years. Marriage was still a viable goal, and with marriage would come the close of my professional career. I did tuck the idea in the back of my mind, however.

While attending summer school at BYU after my third year of teaching, I met a woman with whom a special bond of friendship developed as we shared a home together with two other women. Because of this friendship and because of a new interest in working with children who have learning problems, I asked to be released from my teaching contract. I remained in Provo to pursue a master's degree in educational psychology with an emphasis in learning disabilities. A feeling of concern for others and the desire to serve was developing within me. I received new meaning from my patriarchal blessing that directed me to work with others and to help them solve their problems. After receiving my master's degree, I was hired by Provo School District to work as a resource coordinator in one of the elementary schools.

This change in my life proved to be one of the most challenging I had faced. In California I had been recognized as a leader in Church organizations and had been seen as a strong, capable person. I had felt pretty good about myself, and I had felt quite satisfied with the contribution I was making. In Provo, however, I became acquainted with many self-assured and capable women, and I began questioning my own capabilities as I compared myself with them. My self-concept weakened, and I struggled with self-doubt. I withdrew somewhat and did not contribute during conversations. I was afraid my thoughts and ideas would not be appropriate, that my friends knew so much more and were far more intelligent than I.

My struggle with myself continued for several years until I was able to reverse my thinking pattern and begin identifying my own strengths and qualities that had served me well in the past. Although these were the most difficult years of my life, they were also the most memorable and significant because I learned so much about myself.

I learned that my self-concept in the past had been based on what others thought about me and what I was able to accomplish. As long as others thought I was acceptable and capable, I felt I was. When I was with a group of individuals who seemed more capable, I felt less secure. I judged my self-worth on what I could or could not do compared to them, rather than on who I was. As I came to this understanding, I learned to be more accepting of myself for who I am and to focus on my strengths rather than on my weaknesses. I also learned that others who appear confident and more capable frequently are struggling to overcome their own feelings of inadequacy. There are still moments of doubt, but what I learned then gives me strength now, which helps me through moments of weakness.

While working in Provo School District, I met a woman who supported and encouraged me professionally and personally. She became my friend and advocate and gently pushed me into experiences where I would stretch and grow through committee work and leadership assignments. She believed in me and encouraged me, and I began to feel more secure and to reach out to try new experiences.

At her encouragement, I decided to take evening classes at BYU and receive my administrative endorsement. I had retrieved from the back of my mind the little thought planted by my first principal about serving in a similar position. I decided to prepare for that possibility should I decide in the future to pursue a principalship or an administrative position in the district office.

This was the beginning of many more changes that were to occur in my life. Considering how risky change is, and how unsure the future often is when change occurs, I am surprised that I took so many risks in my professional career. I eventually accepted an administrative position in the district office, and three years later, when a principalship opened, the superintendent asked me to apply for the job. This decision required very careful thought on my part, because I would be going into a situation where there were deep loyalties to the previous principal. I accepted the assignment and was immediately confronted with hostile parents and angry faculty members who felt the transfer of their principal was unfair. There were days when I wondered if anyone liked me or if the position was worth the deep emotional drain which frequently occurred. At the end of the first year, I seriously questioned remaining in the position. I had discovered, however, that I had the strength and ability to meet people, reach out to them, and change their hearts. I was able to separate feelings of anger directed at the position and the situation versus anger directed at me. Feelings were healed, relationships built, and the work progressed.

During my three years as a principal, I several times considered returning to BYU and completing work towards a doctorate in educational administration. Twice I applied and was accepted, and twice I decided not to enroll. The time apparently wasn't right. Finally, in the spring of 1985, I decided to enroll in a doctoral program but not at BYU. I felt I would close some doors if I received my third degree from BYU, although I wasn't sure what those doors would be. Also, the University of Utah had a strong educational administration program, so I applied there and was accepted.

As I accepted each new position in my profession and continued to take classes, I struggled with the idea that I was probably decreasing the odds of my meeting a man who could feel comfortable with a successful professional woman. I also had to face the real possibility that I might never marry and I would have to support myself throughout my life. I decided to continue my growth, both personal and professional, and to take my chances along the way.

I don't consider myself a goal-driven person. Yet with the help and encouragement of family and friends, I made decisions and preparations that opened doors for me as various opportunities arose. I also recognize that I have received guidance and promptings from the Holy Ghost that have blessed my life and increased my capacity to grow and serve.

As I look back, I realize that without considering those decisions as such at the time, I have taken many risks and, therefore, allowed myself to be open to new opportunities. It hasn't been easy. In fact, it has been costly, emotionally and financially. My mission and schooling drained my savings and required many years of study and hard work. I learned that I had to give up one thing in order to gain something greater. I couldn't have everything, but I let my values direct me in what I chose to pursue. My experiences then required me to stretch beyond what was safe, to meet new people, and to take on challenging assignments. In the course of my decisions and experiences, I had determined to make the best of my life whether I remained single or had the privilege of marrying.

Marriage doesn't guarantee happiness. If I do marry, I will take to marriage what I have become while single. And if I never marry in this life, I am a much better and happier person for having developed my talents and having sought to be of service to others. Life is meaningful, productive, and happy if I make it that way. My marital status doesn't make any difference.

What matters is what I do with what I have. My greatest continuing effort is to be a righteous woman, to have the Holy Ghost as a constant companion in my life so that I will be prepared for whatever is to come, be it marriage or continuation as a single person.

The Uncertain Voyage

Joan Okelberry Clissold

The sign, as I sailed past the Point of No Return, said "Uncharted Waters." I had cast off from Married Moorings and was sailing out into the Singles Sea. I knew I would be charting a course new to me, but I thought there would be a manual of instructions for singles just as there had always been a marriage manual, a parenting manual, and other helpful guides. I searched my past issues of the *Ensign*, the Relief Society manuals, and Conference Reports, but there was only a small scattering of comments about how to be single in the married Church of 1972. Although they were helpful, I needed an instruction manual for coping with the day-to-day problems of living as a single woman. I set about learning by trial and error, making notes as I went along.

Becoming single after having been married for a long time caused a prolonged period of adjustment within me. Losing one of life's major roles, that of marriage partner, which I had chosen and enjoyed, compelled me to search for identity all over again. In many ways, it was like being an adolescent. Feelings of pain over the loss and fear of any kind of rejection crowded

---

Joan Okelberry Clissold is the assistant to the president of a health care organization. She earned her bachelor of arts degree in English with a minor in music and art history from the University of Utah. She has filled leadership and teaching positions in Relief Society, Primary, and Young Women. She has also been the trainer of missionary-guides on Temple Square and at the Beehive House.

in continually. As I struggled for answers, the initial overwhelming feelings of inadequacy and separateness were slowly replaced by knowledge that I was not alone and that others felt as I did. I realized that I did not deserve or need to be treated in a special way but rather that I needed to search for myself in new ways. It was like suddenly being stripped of all identities. Who was I? Why did I feel that I was an incomplete person? Why did I feel that because I was no longer married, I also might not be a capable mother or a worthwhile friend? How was I to redefine myself and my relationships with others? These questions were paramount at that time. During the initial part of my effort to cope with being single, self-absorption and self-pity hovered nearby. It became very uncomfortable for me, but I assumed that it was all part of the process of finding clearer self-awareness and increased confidence. I knew it would be a critical period in my life, for decisions made during that adjustment would set the angle of my sails, perhaps for many years.

With my Heavenly Father as my guiding star, the Holy Ghost as my compass, and the scriptures as my maps, I began seeking guidance from the Lord as I had never done before. As I searched back to the beginnings of my faith and testimony, praying earnestly that I would find where I belonged in the eternal plan as a single person, a time of personal revelation came. I felt the Lord's love, and I understood that I was acceptable in his sight, even though I was single and a single parent. At that time, and in recurring periods for some time after, I saw glimpses of my premortal self, that I was strong and good and that the Lord had confidence in me. It was a time of great spiritual awakening; I learned that my lifetime goal to be among his followers would be possible in a new and different way than I had imagined. I also learned much during this time about the use of free agency and dealing with the consequences of using it. My understanding was clarified and heightened, and it gave me new direction to refashion some parts of my life.

For a person who is newly single, the biggest word is *adjustment*. Many normal experiences and contacts feel new and strange. To begin with, attending my own ward seemed like a foreign experience. I had heard about this feeling, but I had lived in my ward a long time so I did not expect it to happen to me. But it did. Feelings of estrangement arose from deep within me. I looked around at the familiar surroundings and people, and I recognized the hymns that were being sung, but I felt like a stranger, almost detached, looking on this experience but not being a part of it. I knew that it had to do with me and not with those surrounding me. I recognized that it was my problem, but I did not know what to do about it. I went home week after week, knowing that I was not an outsider but feeling like one. I prayed about this feeling, what it meant, what I was to learn from it, and how I should react to it. I had heard that for some newly single people, the feeling of alienation is so strong that they leave their ward and turn to other sources for their spiritual guidance.

One Sunday as I left the chapel, I threaded my way through groups of people chatting with one another and went out the door. No one even noticed me. I did the same thing the next week. Yes, I saw that it was possible to come and go without a friendly contact, but I also realized that I had made some effort to avoid others and had been unfriendly myself. I began to realize that if I did not try harder to feel at home, I might develop permanent feelings of being odd or just not fitting in. I could see that it was going to be necessary to put forth a different effort than I had put forth in the past. I would need to help not only myself but others feel comfortable with my single status.

It is hard for married couples in a ward to understand just how the single members fit in or what they are interested in, and so without really meaning to do it, they often leave singles out. For example, the sign-up sheet on the foyer table said: "Marriage relations class—interested couples, please sign up." My single friend and I signed up. I think that the couples in the class wondered what we were doing there on that first day, but they decided not to ask us. We stayed and enjoyed learning by observing the interaction between the other class members, and we also appreciated the feeling of integration with ward members that it gave to us.

A friend of mine lives in a ward where the elders quorum regularly forgets to invite her to social events. Another friend lives in a ward where she is invited but no one offers to pick her up, leaving her to decide whether she wants to go alone to a mainly couples event. I remember feeling grateful to a married couple in my ward who invited me to the first social event I attended as a single person. I felt awkward and nervous—such a funny feeling to have among people I had known for a long time—and I was glad to be identified with these friends for the evening. It was a feeling of great personal accomplishment when the time came that I felt confident enough to attend functions without leaning on anyone for support. Instead of feeling like half of a couple, I finally felt I was of value as a single person.

It is important to let single people in a ward feel part of the whole without thinking that they must do everything like married people or do nothing at all.

One year our Relief Society leaders asked a single woman to plan the annual party. An idea to have a dinner dance was greeted with enthusiasm. I was asked to help with the planning, and we eagerly began preparations. We were rather taken aback one day when a married sister in the ward commented to us that she thought the idea of a dinner dance was a good one, but she asked, "Who are you two going to dance with? (Translation: Not my husband.) She had missed the point. We wanted to plan an event that most of the members could enjoy. We were not thinking of how we would be entertained. Our enjoyment in this event was planning it for others. Even with opportunities to be part of a group, truly fitting in with the married population of the ward or the neighborhood or among married friends is an ongoing effort. Setbacks do occur, sometimes suddenly and at unexpected moments. It is then that magnified feelings of isolation and rejection return and with them the realization that I am not part of the social mainstream of the Church. These times are discouraging; fitting in does not come naturally.

The following experience illustrates how single people can feel in social situations:

It seemed like an ordinary thing to do. I had been going to wedding receptions for years, and this one was in a neighbor's backyard where I had been before. I dressed for the reception and walked down the block and around the side of the house toward the backyard. As I stepped into the backyard I saw the reception line on the far side. The distance suddenly looked as long as a football field, and I was about to walk it by myself. There have been few moments when I have felt so alone, so strange, so out of place. My mind said that these were my neighbors chatting with each other in groups of two and four and six. Why did I feel like a stranger? It was a very long walk across that lawn. I felt separate and apart from everyone. Somehow, I greeted those in the reception line and for those few moments was a part of the festivities, but drifting out of the other end of the wedding party, I was again overwhelmed with feelings of discomfort. I did talk with a few others, but soon found my way out the side yard and fled home alone.

I have thought of that experience many times since and even told it jokingly, much later, to my friends as an example of how strange singleness can make one feel. I talked to myself about it, also. I decided that if I would gather my strength and confidence and go places alone when it was necessary that it would become easier each time and I would get used to seeing people and mingling with others without feeling that I needed someone by my side. When I was married, I had gone places without my husband, but it was not the same. I had always given a reason for my husband's not being there, and thus, even though he was absent, he was there in spirit and in the conversation. Being single, I was simply there, and so I hoped that I would fit in without making others feel responsible for me or without feeling uncomfortable myself. "Just give it time," I used to whisper bravely.

Having been married, I found that maintaining friendships with married couples as a single person brought with it some challenges. As an example, while I was married, there were times when we couples would go out together. During the course of the evening, I would walk arm in arm with the other husband, having a friendly chat. Now, as a single, I found that this is no longer entirely acceptable; walking arm in arm in the same friendly way might be misconstrued as flirtatious and inappropriate. But in a few dear and durable friendships with couples who trust my heart, warm interactions still enrich our bond. Such couples who are able to comfortably integrate me into their lives help me maintain my social balance.

Another big adjustment was learning to date again. Friends were helpful, even though it was hard for them to know just how to go about it. Some were reluctant to make introductions, fearing the relationship might not work out well. I have explained to my friends that the only thing single people need is the introduction. We can take it from there. Caring friends still help with my social life and thus nurture my sense of personal worth.

Regrets for past losses and mistakes can be another problem to work out. These kinds of thoughts can pop into my mind at almost any time. They can be dwelt upon too much, or they can be exchanged for something more pleasant. It is a matter of realizing that they are there and then consciously replacing them. I am a believer in trying not to worry about things that have not taken place or that are beyond my control. Of course, that is not always easy, and there still are times when I wish that some situations were different or that I had behaved in a different manner. I try to follow the concept that what I did then was the best I could do, and if I can do it better now, I will. I realize that I should not punish myself for errors of the past when I was doing my best with the knowledge and skills I had at that time. Knowing that I have tried my best is a wonderful friend when feelings of guilt for past errors creep in and threaten to overcome me.

When I first sailed out upon this Singles Sea, I had a crew of four with me. During that early period of adjustment, we had some smooth sailing, some choppy waves, and a few severe storms. All of us had a lot to learn, and we learned from each other through the struggle. We took time to talk to each other and figure out what the meaning of all this was in each of our lives. We relied on the Savior's simple formula: "Trust in the Lord with all thine heart; and lean not unto thine own understanding. In all thy ways acknowledge him, and he shall direct thy paths." (Proverbs 3:5–6.)

One day, as I was walking with my daughter, I wondered out loud why my parents had been called on a mission just when I was feeling I needed them more than ever before. With the spontaneous wisdom children often show, she said to me, "Well, I think they were called away as part of the Lord's plan, so he could see what you could do all by yourself." It was one of those moments when knowledge of the workings of the Spirit flashed across my consciousness. I knew I had received what I call a mini revelation, which gave me fresh insight and new courage to face the struggle alone.

There was another time when completing my goal to graduate from college began to dim in the face of many frustrations, the added responsibility of single parenting, and flagging energy. It was then that my teenage son came to my rescue. He listened to my reasons for considering dropping out of school, and, after I had given all of the good reasons I could think of, he calmly said, "We won't let you do that. You have almost finished something that has been important to you for a long time. Let us do some of the extra work around home while you do the work to graduate."

He surprised me with this strong, supportive reply. I had thought he was so wrapped up in his own activities—his classes, sports, and dates—that he probably had not paid much attention to what his mother was doing. Instead, he had sensed how deeply I felt about graduating, and he was willing to go the extra mile in helping me reach that goal. In the difficult and anxious process of being a single parent, that kind of moment is satisfying in ways that cannot be expressed in words. To see my children's unselfish determination to help me with a personal achievement was a gratifying moment as a mother. I will always be grateful for his encouragement and strength and for the support that all my children gave me at that time. My crew rallied around me, and graduate I did.

There were times when I did not lead wisely as a mother, and we sailed into choppy waters. On some occasions I let my children use persuasion and temper to influence me away from better decisions that might have been made with more time, thought, and effort. These brought consequences with which I was not happy, and I learned some hard, painful lessons. It made me sad that in those instances I did not set a better example of leadership in the home. It was at such times that the responsibility of being a single parent weighed heavily, and it was necessary to step back and say to myself, "You are among the whole group of parents who make mistakes with their children. It is not just because you are single."

As the child-rearing days went by, I knelt in prayer at the end of each one to ask my Heavenly Father questions about what I needed to do for my children. How could I guide them so they could learn the values and beliefs they would need for a successful life on their own? I did not have all the answers to these questions, but answers in the form of creative thoughts and ideas came through prayerful searching. I was grateful for these valuable insights from the Holy Ghost as we navigated the teenage years.

There were tender moments along the way when deep sharing occurred. Each child asked questions about how I felt and what I believed. My answers were the sieve through which they strained their own thoughts, measured their own progress, and figured out how their beliefs and feelings could be brought into harmony with the eternal truths that guided us.

After sailing along for a number of years, the time came for my crew to cast off, one by one, in their own little vessels. My role as a single parent was completed, at least in the sense of having children at home, on board my ship. I looked back on our voyage together, the problems we had solved, the good times we had shared, and I was filled with humility in the survival and pride in the accomplishment.

When the last child sailed off, ripples of a changing tide gently nudged my conciousness, signaling another time for redefinition of myself. I thought I had done all of that rather thoroughly when I set off into the Singles Sea more than a decade earlier. But here were those same feelings again. Who was I now? What was I going to do? How could I be of the best service and worth to those around me, now that the time spent in parenting was available for other activities? How could I use my time well? How would I maintain contact with my newly formed family units without imposing or being a burden to them?

These questions, along with feelings of insecurity that invariably accompany changes, are all part of the empty nest phase of life. They are probably common to almost all mothers but perhaps are more keenly felt by the single mother. These thoughts caused a brief period of unsettledness within me, and I sensed that it was time to develop new goals and priorities. I drew upon lessons learned from my initial experiences with the single life that had taught me I could look past my immediate feelings of discomfort and know that if I were patient with those funny feelings of having lost my footing again, I would gradually rediscover it and some new pieces of myself as well. I knew that my life was changing, that it would be different from what I had become adjusted to, but I was determined that it would be different in good and positive ways. I could extend my faith and work it out.

Keeping a good balance has always been a resolute goal of mine. It is not a natural gift for most people. It is, rather, the result of slow, disciplined effort. I have a favorite scripture on my kitchen windowsill that reads, "Let us lay aside every weight, and the sin which doth so easily beset us, and let us run with patience the race that is set before us." (Hebrews 12:1.) I love the juxtaposition of the words *race* and *patience*. They don't seem to go together, and yet they are just what I feel is needed to balance the momentum in my life.

It is difficult to achieve balance when there are several important *uns* in my life. There is the disappointment of unrealized dreams, the tenuousness of an unknown future, and the poignant and bittersweet emptiness of unshared affection with a mate. There are basic desires within most of us to share the beauty of the moment, to turn to someone else and exclaim, "Did you see that?" or "Wasn't that music beautiful?" or to quietly hold another's hand and not say anything at all. I know that this yearning to share with another in an intimate and loving way is a divine prompting and will be found in that sphere. To be denied it in this earthly life means learning to hold those dreams of living with an eternal partner in abeyance for a future time. That is very hard to do, and it requires effort to value the positive parts of life while finding ways to overcome the transitory moments of loneliness.

Single life has accentuated my philosophy that all of us need interests that can be enjoyed fully with or without companionship. Some interests I pursue that bring their own satisfaction are books, piano, sewing, gardening, and handwork. I also exercise regularly to keep my emotional balance and maintain my physical well-being. In addition to strenuous exercise, I enjoy walking, especially at sunset, which fills me with the quiet beauty of nature and rejuvenates my spirit. Although I find many ways to use my time alone, I welcome visits from family and friends. I love to share good conversation and feelings of affection. At times, the moments of solitude seem long, but if I do not spend too many anxious moments in wanting my desires for company fulfilled on cue, the rhythm of life takes care of the needs for time alone and time together.

I have been very fortunate to have meaningful and fulfilling work to do in a company whose basic product is service to others. When I was offered my present job, I made it a matter of prayer for several months, trying to decide if I should leave a position I enjoyed to accept the new job. I received an answer to my prayers; I did make the change, all the while feeling rather insecure but still knowing that it was the right thing to do. It has been one of the greatest blessings in my life to be able to work with people who have strong integrity and goals in harmony with mine.

It is also helpful to have activities outside of my work in which I am expected to participate and contribute. Being involved in the community brings me into contact with many different people and helps me keep a good perspective on my life.

A helpful guideline for me in sorting out where singles belong, in the Church and in society in general, is to avoid considering myself unique. As I look around me, I see there are others my age and in my general circumstances; there are those who are older and younger, probably going through similar thoughts and trials as I, at least in some degree. I try to view myself as part of the whole, within the Church and within society, and if I sometimes view singleness as a handicap, then I think, "Doesn't each of us have, by the very nature of our education on earth, one or more of them from time to time?"

When I begin to feel different in negative ways because of my single status, I try to focus on the many ways I am similar to others. It is very easy to get into the habit of punching holes in my self-esteem, becoming waterlogged, and feeling like I am sinking. At times like that, I pause and remember that I can ask and receive a reply, I can seek and find new strength, I can knock and new doors of understanding will open.

As I have tried to encourage other single women, I have also reminded myself that the Lord knows us, our feelings, our dreams, our disappointments. He has work for us to do, and we should strive to know it and be about it. It is not that singles have all the problems and the married people around us are sailing along well. It is that we have problems and challenges different from those of married people, and we will not entirely understand their problems, nor they ours. It is important to guard against being disappointed in not being fully understood. I try not to ask from others what they are not able to give, but rather, I try to enjoy what is within their power and ability to offer. It is comforting to share life's experiences with those who are going through similar events, and those times I cherish; it is also broadening and instructive for me to talk with those who have experiences different from mine. I avoid comparing myself and my situation to others' because I have found that it usually brings either a return to self-pity or a false sense of my own importance. I have had a little quotation taped to my cupboard for a number of years now that never seems to lose its power to help me keep a healthy perspective on my life. It says: "Remember, contentment is not the fulfillment of what you want but the realization of what you already have." I have used that thought many times in keeping myself on a steady course between striving for the future and being at peace with the present.

One of the most difficult adjustments for me as a single person was to find meaning in the role I play rather than wishing for a different role. This was particularly hard because I wanted and enjoyed marriage. I had never even entertained the possibility of being single. While I continue to be sustained by the expectation of marriage and an eternal partnership, I have come to appreciate and enjoy the different dimensions single life affords. Feeling secure in the marriage covenant, I was aware of the responsibility for my exaltation, although my emphasis in achieving this goal was mainly through my roles as wife and mother. Now, it is much clearer to me that exaltation is an individual process, achievable through a variety of roles.

Single life has also provided me with equal, and perhaps more, opportunities to feel the Lord's hand in my life and to develop my ability to respond to promptings and guidance. I enjoy peace of mind as I live my life as a single woman, understanding that to be a disciple of the Savior means that I will be obedient to his will and follow his timetable for the fulfillment of my dreams.

As I continue my voyage, a personalized manual of instructions has evolved to which I keep adding entries. What inlets will there be for me to explore in the future? What new opportunities lie just over the horizon? I will follow my Compass, trim my sails, look up to my Guiding Star, and sail on.

Index